SACRED *of* HAVENS
BROOKLYN

SPIRITUAL PLACES
& PEACEFUL GROUNDS

TERRI COOK

Charleston | London

THE
History
PRESS

Published by The History Press
Charleston, SC 29403
www.historypress.net

Front cover: Stained-glass panel in Red Hook Pentecostal Church. Steeple of the Cathedral
of St. James.
Back cover: First Congregation Anshe Sfard. Dorje Ling Buddhist Center. Japanese Pond
Torii Gate in the Botanic Gardens. Trinity Tabernacle of Gravesend.

All photographs by the author unless otherwise noted.

First published 2013

Manufactured in the United States

ISBN 978.1.60949.982.2

Library of Congress CIP data applied for.

This book is lovingly dedicated to the family of Arthur C. Kentler (1927–2000) and his twin sister, Jeanne Kentler Flaherty (1927–2001), whose Brooklyn roots are engraved on the façade of the Kentler Art Gallery in Red Hook, which was built as the family dry goods store in 1854.

And with gratitude to my family and friends, to librarians and archivists and to those who care for spiritual places.

Contents

CONTENTS

CONTENTS

7

CONTENTS

CONTENTS

Contents

Introduction

Many say that Brooklyn's diversity is reflected in clusters of ethnic restaurants and multiple styles of architecture. I believe its distinctness lies in its sacred havens, and I invite you to come along for a more enlightened tour, discovering Brooklyn through the eyes of its churches, synagogues, temples and public gardens—historic sites that anchor neighborhoods and celebrate the deep spiritual roots of immigrant settlers and their descendants.

Visit churches and graveyards from 1654 developed by the Dutch, who named Breuckelen (meaning "marshland") after a Netherlands village. The first Roman Catholic church, Cathedral of St. James, has witnessed two centuries of Brooklyn's growth from the same site. Sanctuaries, built by freed black slaves, functioned as safe houses and evolved as pivots for social activism. This book will guide you to public parks that restore harmony to the spirit, Buddhist temples filled with peace and Jewish sects with nearly 150 public synagogues—and almost as many in private homes. Learn about havens that help assimilate Hispanic and Caribbean worshipers into American culture and tour Arab havens for the Christian Rite and mosques that call Moslems to prayer five times a day.

When three bridges were opened to Brooklyn, land was readily available, busy waterfronts offered jobs and the lure of healthier living and salty breezes attracted many from crowded Manhattan tenements. Migrants thrived where they could freely work and worship, and in thanksgiving for these fundamental American rights, these settlers built more than two thousand spiritual places, which they utilized not only for solemn rituals but also as social and cultural centers, thus elevating Brooklyn to become the borough of churches.

Part I

Carlmelo Booc.

Downtown Brooklyn

"A nd you that shall cross from shore to shore years hence are more to me, and more in my meditations, than you suppose." These words, from "Crossing Brooklyn Ferry," recall Walt Whitman's spiritual love of humanity but also pay homage to a mode of transport that inspired artists and offered lifelines to early settlers. In the coming years, bridges, highways and trains would do likewise, bringing impressive growth to the city of Brooklyn, which would merge with New York City in 1898. Its downtown neighborhood, always the industrial center and governing seat, remains filled with courthouses, commercial offices and its own Borough Hall, all of which reflect the evolution of Brooklyn's immigrants. Descendants would move to suburbia, leaving their ancestors' history rooted in the area's buildings, especially its sacred havens.

The former Bridge Street Church (see Bedfort-Stuyvesant), constructed in 1846 as the First Free Congregational Church, is now Polytechnic Institute's student center. In spite of the major revitalization of MetroTech and Renaissance Plaza, spiritual places have persevered and continue to welcome newcomers to this historic district bustling with activity and enduring memories of the ferryboat that was once synonymous with downtown Brooklyn. Be sure to visit Walt Whitman Park (Cadman Plaza East and Adams Street) to see more of the native son's words engraved on the façade of a granite fountain.

THE CATHEDRAL BASILICA OF ST. JAMES

During the eighteen century, Brooklyn Roman Catholics would travel by ferry to St. Peter's Church on Barclay Street, Manhattan's first Roman Catholic parish, built in 1785. In turn, Reverend John Power visited commuters, held services in their homes and, during 1818, celebrated the first public Mass in "Irish Town," at Purcell's Inn on York and Gold Streets (also known as Vinegar Hill).

Peter Turner, a local grocer, would head a lay committee to purchase the present property, and the congregation, along with Bishop John Connolly from St. Patrick's Old Cathedral in Manhattan, dedicated the first church on Long Island in 1823. An academic school was followed by a Sunday school, but the church would not be without controversy.

Father John Farnan of Ireland, assigned as the first pastor in 1825, wanted to establish an independent American Catholic Church with no allegiance to Rome. He soon left St. James for his new venture, which evolved into a financial disaster. After the bank foreclosed on the property, the fifth New York archbishop, John Hughes, took control and suspended the radical priest, eventually sending him to Detroit. In 1842, Farnan's building would be dedicated as the Church of the Assumption (see Brooklyn Heights).

Patron James holding the church building.

In about 1845, many Irish immigrants affected by famine conditions crowded into Brooklyn, contributing to the church's enormous growth and necessitating the creation of the Diocese of Brooklyn by Pope Pius IX in 1853. Since it would have its own bishop, St. James Church was designated a cathedral (from the Latin *cathedra*, "chair of the bishop") as the seat of Irish-born John Loughlin (1817–1890), Brooklyn's first bishop. He had been pastor of St. Patrick's Old Cathedral in Manhattan and would serve the new diocese for thirty-eight years, skillfully planning church, school and hospital buildings.

Land was soon purchased for a grander cathedral, and St. James was temporarily assigned as *pro-cathedra* ("in place of"). Since money was always prioritized for schools and hospitals, the new cathedral on Clermont Avenue had to be cancelled, and it became the site of Bishop Loughlin High School. (St. James returned to full cathedral status only in 1972.) Continuous growth would see the diocese divided in 1957 into Kings and Queens Counties, including Staten Island, and Nassau and Suffolk Counties as the new Diocese of Rockville Center.

Pope John Paul II's visit on his first trip to America in 1979 is remembered with a copper plaque on the exterior church wall. Look inside the narthex (the lobby) for a rare decree from Rome in 1982 designating the cathedral as a basilica, an honorary title meaning historically or liturgically important. Official symbols of the tintinnabulum (a small bell) and ombrellino (papal head covering) were installed in 1997 by Bishop Thomas V. Daily, who chose *In Finem Dilexit Eos* ("He Loved Them Even to the End") as the diocese motto. See also the Latin inscription engraved on the marble baldachin (canopy) over the altar table.

In 2003, upon the retirement of Bishop Daily, who served for thirteen years, Nicholas A. DiMarzio Jr. was appointed the seventh bishop. Since size is not a factor for a cathedral, and St. James's pews can seat only several hundred, large celebrations are held at Our Lady of Perpetual Help in Sunset Park (see Sunset Park), where Father DiMarzio was formerly installed as bishop.

Architecture

The historic church, whose site is still surrounded by red brick walls and the traditional cemetery, was designed by John Walters, a local architect from York Street, who won the design competition. In 1846, an addition worked on by architect Patrick Keely was built on the back of the church, necessitating the covering of some headstones. Look for an exterior bust of lay founder Peter Turner near the cemetery, where more than seven thousand were interred between 1823 and 1849.

The present Neo-Georgian façade, with the copper steeple, was yet another addition, in 1903, by architect George H. Streeton. The red brick and terra-cotta exterior, with a gilded sculpture of the patron tucked into a high niche, has a street-level entrance leading into a serene, cream-colored interior. Note the decorative door handles with black metal scallop shells, a symbol of James derived from the pilgrimage site of Compostela, where he's honored as spiritual leader of Spain.

An unadorned vaulted ceiling and cruciform floor plan add to the openness and light of the nave (main sanctuary). In the transept, study the huge medieval-like windows enhanced by Corinthian columns and angel medallions from the Franz Mayer Company in Munich, Germany. They hold the history of the doctrine of the Immaculate Conception, celebrated by the congregation in 1904. Formal proclamation of the dogma was made in 1854 by Pope Pius IX, whose image in the lower window is surrounded by Vatican clergy. Alongside, see a colorful window of Patron James holding a church, perhaps representing the first Catholic church on Long Island. When you leave, stop next door at McLaughlin Park, a welcoming tree-lined space named for early civic leader Hugh McLaughlin Jr. (1823–1904), who fought for Brooklyn to remain a city.

250 Cathedral Place (between Jay and Tillary Streets), Brooklyn, NY 11201; 718-852-4002

CONGREGATION MOUNT SINAI

Chevra Mount Sinai, a Conservative Jewish congregation founded on May 8, 1882, held meetings in private homes and rented halls until it could purchase its first building on State Street in 1909. Moving several times, the group arrived on this site in 1982 that was part of Cadman Towers, a huge apartment complex built as urban renewal in 1973 by Glass & Glass and Conklines & Rossant. Cadman Plaza was named in 1939 for a local minister and the first radio preacher, Reverend S. Parkes Cadman (1864–1936), who strongly opposed racial intolerance. Longtime residents remember the spot as Old Fulton Street, which led to Fulton Ferry Landing, recognized today as New York City's first commercial district.

The beige exterior of the modern synagogue echoes the concrete façade of the complex. A spacious interior, with moveable seating, focuses on a sacred ark encased in wood paneling with gilded-striped doors. Small golden crowns, emblems of the Lions of Judah, adorn the ark, while twelve diminutive crests symbolizing Jewish ethics and rituals fill the facing walls.

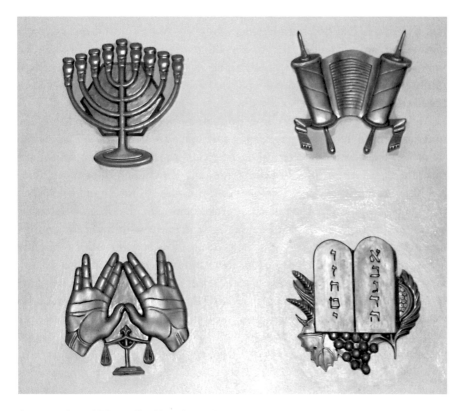

Congregation of Mount Sinai interior wall crests.

See the shofar, the ram's horn blown on New Year and Yom Kippur (day of atonement); the Passover matzo (unleavened bread), with the wine cup commemorating the exodus from Egypt; and the hands of the spiritual leader extended in blessing, the only accepted representation of the human body.

On the sides of the sanctuary, a pair of tall, modern menorahs, seven-branched candleholders with slim brass columns, represents the seven days of creation. They are a reminder of how traditional symbols evolve into modern times yet still represent ancient rituals, not unlike the congregation.

250 Cadman Plaza West (Clarke and Clinton Streets), Brooklyn, NY 11201; 718-875-9124

DORJE LING BUDDHIST CENTER

A bright red entrance gate welcomes visitors into a brilliant yellow building that was once a gas station. The site was purchased in 1989 and renovated as a Buddhist haven in the Vinegar Hill Historic District. Former landowner Jack Johnson named the area after a lost Irish rebellion against the British in County Wexford during 1798. The neighborhood was also called "Irish Town" for the crowds of immigrants living in row houses and working nearby in the Brooklyn Navy Yard, which stayed in operation from 1806 to 1966.

To all who visit this sanctuary, a welcome is extended by monks, who place their hands together and bow their heads in greeting. On the exterior roof, see the Wheel of Doctrine, a universal symbol whose spokes represent the eightfold path of Buddhism. Founded and directed by Venerable Tashi Gyaltsan Rinpoche from Tibet, the center has a main hall, which focuses on the altar's towering, golden Buddha statue wrapped in a saffron-colored robe. Glass cases are filled with smaller Buddhas, while colorful banners hang from the walls. The altar is usually crowded with offerings, including fruit, lighted candles and flowers. Featured is a photo of the Dalai Lama (Universal Teacher), while incense is left to thank the deity, who helps a Buddhist eliminate illusions about life.

Buddha (Sanskrit for "the enlightened one") is said to have been born of nobility in Nepal and to have lived from 563 BC to 483 BC. His life story, written two hundred years after his death, is shrouded by legend, but his basic philosophy is well recorded. There were also no graven images of Buddha until the fourth century AD. His early followers would use the stupa, a dome-shaped monument, to remember their teacher. Buddha was concerned with

Altar of Dorje Ling Buddhist Center.

human sorrow and suffering in the lives of ordinary people. He felt that these emotions could be overcome by giving up personal ambition and selfishness and practicing moderate detachment. The goal was a complete state of bliss or spiritual awakening known as nirvana, which brought the end of rebirth (samsara). Buddhists believe that to be reborn in another body is to suffer, repeatedly, the problems of humanity.

Buddhism originated in India and rapidly spread throughout the Far East as the silk route traders introduced its principles to China and Southeast Asia. Three branches developed: Theravada, Mahayana and Vajrayana, all with many sects. A different emphasis on Buddha's original philosophy is practiced by each sect, but all Buddha images, be they jolly or austere, teach the way to virtue. Since enemies are met with compassion, peace is the only possibility. Don't miss the courtyard, which holds colorful prayer flags (dar cho) that are guided by the wind and transport petitions to heaven. The center is open daily.

98 Gold Street (between Front and York Streets), Brooklyn, NY 11201; 718-522-6523

CHURCH OF THE OPEN DOOR

This low, modern red brick sanctuary has a prominent Christian cross mounted on an elongated steeple that seems to reach up to the nearby Brooklyn-Queens Expressway. Encircled by a garden, the church was designed in 1954 by Adams & Woodbridge and is well known for an open-door policy that welcomes all to services, hence its name.

Farragut Houses, a ten-building city project completed in 1952 on sixteen acres, towers over the church and dominates the neighborhood. The complex is named for David Farragut (1801–1870), who was a Spaniard by birth and became the first admiral of the U.S. Navy during the Civil War. He is fondly remembered for his quote "Damn the torpedoes, full speed ahead!"—not unlike this church, which participates determinedly in programs for reformation of public education, prison ministries and the propagation of black heritage.

The serene interior, with a warm vaulted ceiling of wood, is focused on a simple cross above the pastor's pulpit, where progressive Christianity is preached both from current events and the Bible. Wooden pews seat two hundred congregants, who continue to play an important community role in their Vinegar Hill neighborhood, which witnessed the negative side of growth. Construction of the Manhattan Bridge in 1909 dissected the area, Con Edison built a power plant on its waterfront in the 1920s and streets disappeared in the 1950s for entrance ramps leading to the Brooklyn-Queens Expressway. Due to strong community intervention, what remained of Vinegar Hill was declared a historic district in 1997.

201 Gold Street (and Nassau Street), Brooklyn, NY 11201; 718-643-1081

THE ORATORY CHURCH OF ST. BONIFACE

In 1853, a group of German Roman Catholics that had settled near the East River received a donation of $100 from Reverend Joseph A. Schneller, pastor of St. Paul's Church (see Cobble Hill), to purchase St. Thomas Episcopal Church. The congregation, outgrowing the space, built this sanctuary, designed by Patrick C. Keely, in 1872 on this nearby site, dedicating it to the patron saint of Germany while continuing sermons in German until the 1920s.

Over the years, rapid changes in demographics found St. Boniface in the middle of a commercial area with almost no permanent congregation. Today, the church personifies the gentrification of its MetroTech neighborhood named after the development company, and it has been revived by huge numbers of commercial tenants and new residents moving into the busy downtown area.

Three entrance doors and asymmetrical copper steeples topping off exterior twin towers complement the Early Gothic red brick building. A rectangular interior, remodeled after fire damage in the 1950s and again in the 1990s, focuses on the apse's simple altar table and a huge wooden cross from Italy. High above the cross, an original triangular-shaped stained-glass window was restored after the 1990s fire due to the sensitive rescue of damaged pieces by the New York City Fire Department.

German prayer in stained glass at the Oratory Church of Saint Boniface.

Moveable cane chairs can seat six hundred, while an original marble baptismal font with a unique copper cover has been placed at the church's entrance signifying baptism as the entry into Christian life. Green scagliola (artificial marble) Corinthian columns line the cream-colored sanctuary like tall, decorative trees, while engraved glass walls divide the nave from the shrine-filled narthex. Walk around the sanctuary's perimeter to see a modern interpretation of the Stations of the Cross (the story of Jesus's death) in fourteen glass-tempered panels embedded in oak flooring.

Look up to the clerestory level, where instead of stained glass you'll see original murals of the apostles, the twelve disciples selected by Jesus to spread his teachings; these icons are often found in German churches. Be sure to study the colorful windows surviving from the founding congregation, especially the pair inscribed in old German that holds images of the Patron Boniface (AD 609–755) as preacher and a description of his martyrdom caused by proselytizing long before there would be a united Germany. An angel displays an inscribed scroll that translates, "Travel the world and teach all the people." Boniface managed to travel and establish many churches and remains the favorite saint of German beer brewers. Also see the images of St. Philip Neri (1515–1595) over the side door entry and at a small shrine. In about 1564, Philip put together an oratory in Rome, a small community of religious people that would serve the area where they lived. Oratorians are often lauded for their reading of scripture and joyful singing, and under the title of Oratory of St. Philip Neri, they have been ministers at St. Boniface's since 1990. The oratory is open daily from 7:00 a.m. to 2:00 p.m.

190 Duffield Street (between Willoughby and Myrtle Avenues), Brooklyn, NY 11201; 718-875-2096

STS. CONSTANTINE AND HELEN GREEK ORTHODOX CATHEDRAL

Roman emperor Constantine (circa AD 280–337), after defeating the forces of Maxentius and upon his own conversion in AD 312, moved his empire and rebuilt the ancient Greek city-state of Byzantium, renaming it Constantinople. He declared Sunday a public holiday and organized the Council of Nicaea in AD 325, where the Nicene Creed was endorsed as a unified statement of beliefs. It remains a vital part of Christian ritual.

Helen, the mother of Constantine, was made dowager empress by her son even though she remained in York, England, until her death in AD 328. While on a tour of Golgotha in the Holy Land, following a grandson's death, Helen is said to have discovered the true cross of Christ and inspired the building of Holy Land churches at the site of the Nativity, the Holy Sepulchre and the Ascension.

Constantinople suffered its final fall to Turkey in 1453. In the post-Byzantine world, Greece remained under Ottoman rule until it won independence in 1830, but the artistic legacy of Byzantium would continue to be reflected in Greek churches, icons and architecture.

In 1916, this Greek immigrant congregation, founded in 1913 on nearby Lawrence Street, dedicated the cornerstone for Brooklyn's first Greek Orthodox church and named the sanctuary in honor of revered patrons of Christianity. Since there were few Greek churches and no diocese in the United States, the church charter had to be issued from Greece. In 1966, the sanctuary was elevated to a higher status—look in the apse (altar area) for the archbishop's gilded chair, a symbol that you are in a cathedral. The Greek Archdiocese of the United States was started in the church basement during 1916 and flourished along with the church.

Architecture

The beige brick cathedral reflects all of the design elements of Byzantine architecture: the cross-in-square interior, a central dome, round arches and a jewel-box decor filled with traditional icons. Its bell tower was a new addition in 1992.

The five-hundred-seat sanctuary was severely damaged by fire in 1991, necessitating a complete interior restoration designed by Peter Papadatos & Associates. Round-arch windows are uniquely filled with white textured wood perforated with small circles of amber glass. The original iconographer in 1948, Constantine Youssis, along with his associate Kostos Skordelos, once again created icons and murals to embellish the interior's walls, ceilings and arches.

Because icon production was wisely moved from Constantinople to Crete during the fifteenth and sixteenth centuries, this religious art form survived all uprisings and wars. It is characterized by frontal presentations of images looking out from heavenly heights and with golden backgrounds representing the light in God's kingdom. Look up to the interior's center dome and see the most famous icon, *Christ Pantocrator (Great High Priest)*, along with a huge, golden-filigree chandelier with small bulbs resembling hundreds of candles.

In the apse, an iconostatis (wooden gate painted with icons) holds the Holy Door, through which only clergy may enter to celebrate at the altar. See also the image of Constantine and Helen. Above the altar, an enormous Byzantine mural of Mary holding the child Jesus acknowledges the elevated role of women among Christians. Seven lamps, which can be traced to ancient churches and synagogues, gently illuminate the sacred area. Upon entering the sanctuary, visitors often light cream-colored candles that cast a transcendent glow throughout this regal haven.

64 Schermerhorn Street, Brooklyn, NY 11201; 718-624-0595

BROOKLYN TABERNACLE

This skillfully restored sanctuary was a former Loews movie theater designed in 1903 by Thomas Lamb. It was boarded up in the 1990s until this Christian ministry, centered in contemporary gospel music, purchased the property in 1998. The congregation of more than eight thousand had several Brooklyn homes before relocating to this site in 2002, and it utilizes its wide stage to feature a large choir and a backdrop of an iconic image of the Holy Spirit with the statement, "God Is Love."

Although gospel music has crossed over to popular culture, its message is still the story of faith and salvation through Jesus Christ. Its growth can be traced to the Pentecostal movement that began in the southern part of the United States in about 1900, when worshipers wanted emotional involvement added to their services.

Migrants would bring their music with them and influence many Brooklyn churches that once had only formal choirs. Sanctuaries started to include gospel music in the 1930s, and concerts soon spread throughout the country. Clarence Taylor, in *The Black Churches of Brooklyn*, wrote that some two thousand people attended a national convention of gospel choral groups in 1941 at Bridge Street AWME (see Bedford-Stuyvesant)—hence the need for large spaces.

The church's main auditorium seats more than three thousand. Besides meditating, there is another reason to raise your eyes to the heavens: a grandiose ceiling centered with an original dome and a crystal chandelier.

Former theater seats are covered in brocade, and woodwork was restored with gilded touches. Brass grills hold musical angels, while handsome gold frames highlight lobby paintings. See a traditional river baptism or a country preacher holding services in a small church.

The new red brick exterior has two entrances: one located in busy Fulton Mall and another around the corner on Smith Street. The Fulton Street lobby also has murals that are representations from Psalm 23 ("The Lord is my shepherd") and Psalm 100 ("Acclaim the Lord, all men on earth").

This gospel choral group won a 1996 Grammy Award, a recognition of excellence from the music industry. Remember that with such an outstanding choir and a large congregation, seats fill up fast, an impetus to get to church on time.

17 Smith Street (between Fulton and Livingston Streets), Brooklyn, NY 11201; 718-290-2000

FRIENDS MEETINGHOUSE

Well known for emphasizing the "Inner Light," a feeling of God's guiding spirit within each body, this Christian congregation gathers without a formal minister but with the Bible as its guide, in a haven that stresses equality, peace and service to others.

The Religious Society of Friends began in England in the seventeeth century when a group led by George Fox (1624–1691) sought direct communion with God and left the Anglican Church. Fox instructed his group to tremble before the word of the Lord, and the mocking title of Quakers arose from this quaking or shaking during worship.

When a group of English Friends settled on farms around Long Island in 1657, the members were persecuted by the Dutch. After filing a protest—*The Flushing Remonstrance*, which demanded religious tolerance—they were jailed by the New Amsterdam government. The Friends were better tolerated under British rule and continued their ministry devoted to moral causes and pacifism. One of their early cemeteries still exists in Prospect Park.

In 1835, the first Brooklyn Heights meetinghouse was built at the corner of Henry and Clark Streets. Outgrowing the space, the group constructed the present landmark site in 1857, a red brick sanctuary set in a bluestone-cobbled courtyard and enclosed within a high wrought-iron fence. Its façade, more than three stories high with five tall windows, rises to a peaked roof with a low gable. The white wooden porch, with an added glass enclosure, has a triangular pediment echoing the roofline.

The simplicity and symmetry of the Greek Revival design, with Italianate details, is attributed to Charles T. Bunting, a well-known builder and member of the Friends who is thought to have constructed similar meetinghouses, including one on East 15th Street in Manhattan.

In the unadorned interior, the only decorative features are twin stairways holding Italianate-design balusters within a wide entrance hall. The second-floor meeting room has original wainscoting topped with plaster walls, as well as white wooden benches thought to have been from the original house. The serene space holds two hundred, with an additional social room seating one hundred, and is available for rental to neighborhood groups. Today, the haven is isolated in the shadow of the Central Court Building across from the New York Transit Museum and in an area designated as the Brooklyn Skyscraper District.

110 Schermerhorn Street, Brooklyn, NY 11202; 718-625-8705

JEWS FOR JESUS

This Conservative organization promotes Messianic Judaism every July with its familiar appearances on Brooklyn's street corners. The movement was started in 1973 in San Francisco by Martin Meyer Rosen (1932–2010), who accepted the Old and New Testaments and promoted the message of salvation through faith in Jesus Christ. The group honors Messiah Y'shua, supports the State of Israel and believes in the power of the Trinity (the doctrine of three persons in one: God the Father, God the Son and God the Holy Spirit). This exclusively Jewish ministry observes Passover and Yom Kippur and quotes an old Yiddish phrase, "Man drives but God holds the reins." Questions are gladly answered at its website, jewsforjesus.org.

109 East 31st Street, New York City, NY 10016; 212-974-8248

THREE BRIDGES

The building of three bridges spanning the East River contributed to the demise of the many ferry lines that were major links between Brooklyn and

Lamplight on Brooklyn Bridge.

Manhattan. By 1924, ferry terminals were obsolete. Automobiles, introduced in 1908, were the popular mode of travel, and with an eye to the future, designers would include motorways in bridge plans.

The Brooklyn Bridge transformed the city of Brooklyn and provided easy access to Manhattan. The public has loved its 1,595.5-foot span since its fourteen-year construction project was completed in 1883. At that time, thirteen ferry lines were crossing the East River. Stand in the middle of the steel-suspension bridge and feel the spirituality and sense of freedom that this landmark inspires. Walt Whitman's poetry is etched on bronze plaques placed under its famous Gothic arches, while the American flag flies high above the granite tower.

Bridge designer John A. Roebling, a Prussian-born civil engineer and the inventor of wire cable, died from lockjaw as the project was beginning. His foot had been crushed by a ferryboat while he was surveying the site. His son and associate, Alexander, became a victim of the bends, an underwater workers' disease caused by a too-rapid ascent to the surface. It fell to Alex's wife, Emily, to finish the plan as her husband watched from their nearby Brooklyn home on Columbia Heights.

Be sure to see the bronze plaque placed by the Brooklyn Engineers Club that reads: "The builders of this bridge dedicated to the memory of Emily Warren Roebling (1843–1903) whose faith and courage helped her stricken husband Col. Washington A. Roebling C. E. (1837–1926) complete the construction of this bridge from the plans of his father John A. Roebling C.E. (1806–1869) who gave his life to the bridge. 'Back of every great work we can find the self-sacrificing devotion of a woman.'"

Emily's bridge has pedestrian and bicycle lanes, with motor traffic on the lower level. Its connection to the business district of Lower Manhattan invited a wealthier class to migrate to nearby neighborhoods. The Brooklyn entrance is at Adams and Tillary Streets in Cadman Plaza, and the Manhattan entrance is across from City Hall Park and Broadway. When walking from Manhattan, watch for an exit on your left and proceed down the stairway to Washington Street. You will be in DUMBO ("Down Under the Manhattan Bridge Overpass") and only three blocks to the East River.

The Manhattan Bridge, designed with two levels by engineer G. Lindenthal, was opened in 1909, with dramatic entrance portals created by Carrére & Hastings. Take the N train over the bridge for an insatiable view of the city as the subway emerges from the East River tunnel. The bridge leads into Flatbush Avenue, a major thoroughfare extending from downtown Brooklyn to Gateway National Park, which holds Floyd Bennett Field, opened in 1931 as the first municipal airport.

Entire residential blocks were demolished for the building of bridges, as well as construction of the Brooklyn-Queens Expressway. DUMBO, between Main and Bridge Streets, received its name in the 1970s from artists who had moved into this desolate area, with vestiges remaining from a tobacco warehouse and retail stores. Small businesses are buzzing again as more artists and real estate developers continue

DUMBO, "Down Under the Manhattan Bridge Overpass."

Manhattan Bridge from Fort Greene Park.

Williamsburg Bridge.

to transform the neighborhood, which was officially recognized as a historic district by the Landmarks Preservation Commission in 2007. Nearby, in Brooklyn Bridge Park, enjoy the Manhattan skyline and quiet meditation on the waterfront.

The Williamsburg Bridge was opened in 1903, attracting the economically deprived migrants fleeing tenements on the Lower East Side of Manhattan. Chief Engineer Leffert L. Buck included train and trolley service in his plans, which started at Delancey Street and led to South 5th Avenue in Williamsburg. Pedestrian paths facilitated an easy return for food and supplies on Manhattan's Orchard Street. The M or J trains are great ways to see the suspension bridge while crossing the East River into a busy neighborhood that is positioned north of both the Brooklyn and Manhattan Bridges.

Brooklyn Heights

R obert Fulton's ferryboat brought not only commuters from Manhattan's Wall Street in twelve minutes but also prosperity to this geographically desirable neighborhood. Businessmen built private homes, developed commercial ventures and dedicated many sacred havens. By 1860, Brooklyn had become the third-largest city in the United States, and the Heights was its architecturally diverse asset, compliments of successful financiers. During the 1960s, local residents would band together to save historic housing that was being razed for both modern apartment buildings and the Brooklyn-Queens Expressway. Commissioner Robert Moses would concede and divert traffic under the Esplanade, a plan that became a model for future development.

The forty-block neighborhood became the first landmark district in 1965 when the New York City Landmark Commission was established, and it symbolizes the importance of historical preservation in an ever-changing city. Spiritual havens are prominently featured within the district and add graceful Gothic touches to the neighborhood's quiet radiance.

BROOKLYN HEIGHTS ESPLANADE

In this raging city, a peaceful promenade made its debut in 1950, bordering the East River for one-third of a mile between Remsen and Orange Streets. This cantilevered spot sits atop the Brooklyn-Queens Expressway, which diverted traffic from residential streets. Commissioner Robert Moses planned this concession after much noise was made by the locals about his destructive original proposal. The esplanade is simply designed with asphalt paving, well-placed seating and green gardens where you can rest your spirit while viewing the Statue of Liberty, the Brooklyn Bridge and the Verrazano Bridge to the south. The World Trade Center, which was lost on September 11, 2001, was highly visible from this spot, and local artists have memorialized the Twin Towers by attaching photos to the railing.

At the Montague Street entrance, see the historic copper plaque that was a gift in 1929 from the Long Island State Society, Daughters of the Revolution, and reads: "This tablet marks the land on which stood, Four Chimneys, the house occupied by General George Washington as headquarters during Battle of Long Island in which the council of war was held August 29, 1776 when it was decided to withdraw the American Army from Long Island."

THE WATCHTOWER BUILDING

Close by the Brooklyn Bridge, this huge complex held the worldwide governing body of Jehovah's Witnesses and other support personnel in tending to their mission of preaching the Bible globally. In April 2012, the congregation, once the largest landholder in DUMBO and Brooklyn Heights, announced long-range plans to move to Warwick, New York, a small town on the New Jersey border. Preservationists and neighbors are sad to see their good neighbors leave because of the many buildings they restored and meticulously maintained.

The Jehovah's Witnesses sect was founded in Pennsylvania in 1870 by Charles Taze Russell and was incorporated in 1884 as the Watch Tower Bible and Tract Society of Pennsylvania. The current name was adopted in 1931. The group, which first came to Brooklyn in 1909, purchased the present site from Squibb Pharmaceutical Company in 1969 and added the iconic Watchtower sign in 1970. The logo is a signal for those who cross from Manhattan that they've landed in the "Twin City," the designation by poet Emma Lazarus (1849–1887) for the ports of Brooklyn and Manhattan.

25 Columbia Heights, Brooklyn, NY 11201; 718-560-5000

CHURCH OF THE ASSUMPTION
OF THE BLESSED VIRGIN MARY

In 1825, Irish-born Father John Farnan was assigned to St. James Roman Catholic Church as its first pastor (see Downtown Brooklyn). In an attempt to break with Rome, he established an independent American Catholic Church at the corner of Jay and York Streets, but it was a financial failure. After the bank foreclosed on the building, it was taken over by Bishop John Hughes, who suspended Farnan, eventually sending him to Detroit.

In 1842, Farnan's sanctuary was dedicated as Church of the Assumption, the fourth Roman Catholic Church in Brooklyn, but that property was declared eminent domain in 1903 and demolished to build the Manhattan Bridge. The city's financial settlement allowed the purchase of the present site, which opened on August 15, 1909, the feast day of the patron.

The Italian Renaissance brick building has all the symmetry identifying its style. A central recessed doorway and two side doors have projecting cornices supported by scroll-shaped brackets. Look for charming angel medallions and a single rounded-arch window on the white façade.

The rectangular interior, with six Corinthian columns supporting round arches, features a decorative barreled-shaped ceiling and a choir loft holding an image of St. Cecilia, patron of music. The nave's stained-glass windows, by F.X. Zettler of Royal Bavarian Art Institute, tell the story of the fifteen mysteries of the rosary, a vocal and meditative prayer on the life of Jesus and his mother, Mary. The assumption of Mary to heaven is featured over the Italian marble altar with a baldachin.

Look in the side chapel for a huge mural of Mary holding the infant Jesus while presenting a rosary to St. Dominic, founder of Order of the Preachers, and St. Catherine of Siena (1347–1380), given the title "Doctor of the Church" and known for her theological work *Dialogue*. Beads are an ancient way to count, but this charming legend of the rosary (a string of ten beads in five sets) remains in Catholic history. The Latin word *rosarium*, meaning rose garden or garland, is appropriate to represent such a distinct devotion to Mary.

In 1990, a baptistery and ambo, which holds sacred oils, were installed along with two shrines as gifts from the Italian Historical Society. Visitors are welcomed through the office at 64 Middagh Street.

55 Cranberry Street, Brooklyn, NY 11201; 718-625-1161

PLYMOUTH CHURCH OF THE PILGRIMS

The Man Who Saved Oregon in stained glass at Plymouth Church of the Pilgrims.

Because of the continuous battle in Presbyterian churches between fundamentalists, who rejected any liberal interpretation of the Bible, and modernists, who sought intellectual freedom, congregations were always splintering and starting new sanctuaries. Two groups are associated with this church: Church of the Pilgrims, formed in 1844, and Plymouth Church (officially, the Third Congregational Church), organized in 1847.

This site was purchased from the First Presbyterian Church by the Plymouth group and included a meetinghouse on Cranberry Street. In 1850, the sanctuary was destroyed by fire and replaced by today's church, built at the front of the Orange Street property. In 1934, Church of the Pilgrims merged with the Plymouth group, leaving its nearby 1844 building that would become Our Lady of Lebanon Maronite Cathedral.

Plymouth's first minister, Henry Ward Beecher (1813–1887), arrived in 1847 and served until his death. He was a fiery preacher with an ambitious agenda: abolish slavery, give women voting rights, enforce temperance and accept Judaism as the third major faith group in America. In the press, he was known as "the cause of the Civil War," while his talented sister, Harriet Beecher Stowe (1811–1896), published her view of slavery in *Uncle Tom's Cabin*.

When Beecher was accused of adultery with a married woman, his reputation was severely damaged, even though he won the jury trial. But his death revealed his lasting influence when public schools and the New York State legislature closed to attend his funeral. The preacher now eternally rests at Green-Wood Cemetery on Dawn Path (see Sunset Park).

Architecture

The red brick Italianate church with Colonial touches was designed in 1849 by English architect Joseph C. Wells; the white entrance porch and stained-glass windows were early twentieth-century additions. With seating for two thousand, the unadorned sanctuary holds cream-colored pews, a balcony supported by cast-iron columns and nineteen figurative windows by Frederick Stymetz Lamb. The images represent American religious, political and intellectual liberty and tell two stories, *The History of Puritanism and Its Influence upon Institutions and People of the Republic* and *The Development of Religious Liberty*. Look for the trio of Marcus Whitman, John Tyler and Daniel Webster in a window donated by James A. Moore of Seattle, Washington, "in grateful recognition of the man who saved Oregon to the Union."

Other windows installed between 1907 and 1909 include *William Penn: Peace Movement of Pennsylvania*, *Thomas Hooker: First Settlement at Hartford*, *The Haystack Meeting: Williams College 1806* and *Evening Prayer: Hugenots in the Carolinas*. Be sure to see a silver plaque marking pew no. 89 to honor the first visit of Abraham Lincoln in 1860, as well as the president's stained-glass image on the balcony wall.

Plymouth's church house and connecting arcade were built in 1913 on Hicks Street by Woodruff Leeming. Hillis Hall, named for Plymouth's third preacher, holds five Tiffany windows belonging to the Pilgrim group that brought them from its former church, along with a piece of Plymouth Rock acquired in 1840. Look for portraits of pastoral leaders, as well as the popular painting of Reverend Beecher auctioning young female slave Pinkie in order to buy her freedom.

Be sure to visit the Orange Street Garden, which holds a massive bronze of Beecher and a bas-relief of Abraham Lincoln, both by Gutzon Borglum of Mount Rushmore fame. The preacher is also fondly remembered as an abolitionist with an imposing sculpture by John Quincey Adams Ward just a short stroll north of Borough Hall.

75 Hicks Street (and Orange Street), Brooklyn, NY 11201; 718-624-4743

DANISH SEAMEN'S CHURCH

Built in the 1850s, this Greek Revival brownstone (also called *Dansk Somands Kirke*) was once the home base for visiting sailors, many of whom permanently settled in the busy port city of Brooklyn. The Danish mariners bell placed in the front garden is a clever way to honor the former residents, as well as to call congregants to service. The original Lutheran sanctuary was started in 1878 on 9th Street in Carroll Gardens by Pastor Rasmus Andersen, who founded many seamen shelters along the New York waterfront. This is the only survivor of that ministry, along with the pastor's portrait, which has a place of honor in the sanctuary.

The present congregation relocated to this residential block in 1957 and welcome all to its independent church, where Danes not only celebrate solemn rituals but also utilize the lower floor and garden for social and cultural events. Crisp white walls and pale wood chairs fill the long, narrow chapel, and models of old ships hang from the sanctuary's ceiling. Above the altar table, a modern stained-glass panel by Danish artisan Maja Lina Engelhardt features *The Risen Christ* as told in the Gospel of John.

102 Willow Street, Brooklyn, NY 11201; 718-875-0042

First Unitarian Church of Brooklyn and Church of the Saviour

First Unitarian Church.

Unitarianism was the nineteenth-century brainchild of William Ellery Channing, a minister of the Federal Street Church in Boston, whose sermon "Unitarian Christianity" was the faith's foundation. Lucy Channing Russel, William's sister, had invited about forty people to her home in Lower Manhattan to hear her brother preach that the Bible must be interpreted by reason, and since it "proclaims the unity of God...We object to the doctrine of the Trinity." The Trinity is a dogma that maintains that one God exists in three divine figures: God the Father, Jesus the Son and the Holy Spirit. The dogma, stated in the Nicene Creed, cannot be explained by reason and is accepted as the center of Christian theology. Channing's sermon, reprinted in pamphlet form, became a bestseller, leading his adherents to establish a Unitarian congregation in Manhattan whose charter dates from 1819. "The Boston religion" spread to Brooklyn via residents who traveled by ferry across the East River to Sunday services.

The First Unitarian Society in Brooklyn was begun in 1833 by several families who held on to their liberal religious views. In 1835, the group purchased the Second Presbyterian Church on Adams Street, with Reverend David Hatch Barlow as pastor. However, disaffected members soon broke away and formed the Second Unitarian Church, only to reunite in 1842 and build the present church on the site that once was a British fort in 1780. Seth Low (1850–1916), mayor of Brooklyn in 1881 and mayor of New York in 1902, was a former president of the congregation.

The Gothic Revival brownstone church, with its many spires, was completed in 1844 by Minard Lafever. An interior nave, seventy-five feet long, has wonderful stained-glass Tiffany opalescent windows from 1890 that fill the east and west sides of the nave; the clerestory level is filled with original painted art glass. For a more intimate area, visit the chapel, added in 1865, and note the cast-iron fence surrounding the exterior of the church, a reminder to the neighborhood of its age.

50 Monroe Place (and Pierrepont Street), Brooklyn, NY 11201; 718-624-5466

CHURCH OF ST. ANN AND THE HOLY TRINITY

Neighbors gathered in 1784 within an abandoned British army barrack at Middagh and Fulton Streets to dedicate their spiritual haven to Ann—the mother of Mary, who bore Jesus—and also honor its generous benefactor, Ann Sands. Dutch Reform churches were prevalent on Long Island at this time, but local British soldiers and officers wanted to worship in a haven resembling the Anglican Church of England. St. Ann's would prosper and outgrow several buildings; the last, designed by Renwick & Sands in 1869, still stands as part of Packer Collegiate Institute on Clinton Street.

Holy Trinity Free Church was organized in 1844 by paper manufacturer Edgar John Bartow and his wife, Harriet Pierrepont, who wished to attract neighbors traveling to Trinity Church in Manhattan. No pew rental was required, hence its designation as a free church. In the 1950s, the parish was dissolved and its building left vacant until St. Ann's congregation moved in and included the former group in its official name. Look in the narthex for an opaque glass window of St. Peter that was dedicated to Thomas Elliott, "housekeeper of the Lord—1855–1885," a fitting remembrance of Holy Trinity members.

Designed by Minard Lafever in 1844 and considered his masterpiece, this Gothic Revival landmark is protected from demolition. It lost its spire in 1905 when it was removed as a hazard; poor-quality brownstone had led to serious exterior problems, and continuing repairs of the plaster interior remains financially challenging. An outstanding feature of this delicate sanctuary has always been its suite of sixty figurative stained-glass windows (circa 1844–48), the first set crafted in America by the English Bolton brothers, William Jay (1816–1884) and John (1818–1898). Scenes from the Old and New Testaments are inspiring. The *Tree of Jesse* depicts ancestors of Jesus, and the chancel window of *The Ascension and Glorification of Jesus* reaches forty feet high over the spire-enhanced high altar. Located behind the pipe organ was the *Miriam & Jubal* window before it was permanently moved to the Metropolitan Museum of Art. The Boltons revived the Renaissance art form of glass painting in America and influenced John La Farge and Louis Comfort Tiffany, whose works are well represented in Brooklyn's sacred havens.

157 Montague Street (and Clinton Street), Brooklyn, NY 11201; 718-875-6960

FIRST PRESBYTERIAN CHURCH

Ezra Woodhull and nine friends met at the Brooklyn Sabbath Union Sunday School in 1822, where they formally organized and successfully planned to build the first sacred haven in Brooklyn Heights on Cranberry Street.

When Brooklyn became a city in 1834, after annexing its five towns—New Amersfoort (Flatlands), Midwout (Flatbush), Boswick (Bushwick), New Utrecht and Gravesend—the official celebration was held in the Cranberry Street sanctuary. The first mayor, George Hall, was a trustee of the church, as well as its choir director.

Dissension always seemed to exist in the Presbyterian Church, and in 1844, there were great conflicts over theology, a proposal to merge with the Congregationalists and the issue of slavery, which would cause disenchanted members to establish the Church of the Pilgrims, while others joined another new group, Plymouth Church.

First Presbyterian continued to grow while supporting the abolition of slavery and dedicated the present site in 1847. The Cranberry Street property was sold to Plymouth Church and its minister, Reverend Henry Ward Beecher.

The brownstone and red brick Gothic Revival church, designed in 1846 by William B. Olmsted, is set within a garden with walking paths and two huge trees. Along one path sits a pair of old Celtic crosses, rescued from a dismantled Methodist church. Look up to the exterior ninety-foot-tall crenellated tower to see stained glass from 1847. A teakwood entrance, completed in 1921 by James Gamble Rogers, bears the inscription on its tympanum, "To the Glory of God in Memory of Henry Rogers Mallory."

Upon entering the narthex, visitors are greeted by the wooden sculpture *Cross of the Common Man*, a gift from Brooklyn artist Rick Niezeig in 1975. The 1,200-seat sanctuary—with an elaborately carved black walnut apse, installed in 1882—has five Tiffany windows, including *The Fisherman* from 1882 and *The River of Life* from 1921. A trustee, Willis Lord Ogden, and his wife are remembered with a view of the Ausable River in the Adirondacks, where they spent their summers.

The founding congregation had forbidden decorative furnishings and musical instruments, but with the increase in more liberal members, a sparsely furnished interior would gradually fill with artifacts to inspire the eye as well as the heart. In 1883, the marble baptismal font and carved black walnut pulpit were installed, along with a new organ. Today, music is a prerequisite of all Presbyterian churches, and in this sanctuary, services are celebrated with traditional hymns, as well as songs of gospel, rock and jazz. When visiting during the week, enter through the parish house.

124 Henry Street, Brooklyn, NY 11201; 718-624-3770

Zion German Evangelical Lutheran Church

In December 1855, a small group of German immigrants, with hopes to preserve their Lutheran heritage, worshiped with Pastor Friedrich W.T. Steimle in a rented hall at Nassau and Fulton Streets. In 1856, they purchased the present building, which had been constructed as a Dutch Reformed church in 1839 but was used as a concert hall.

The congregation's formal name, Deutsche Evangelical Lutheran Zion's Rirrhe, is engraved on the portico of the red brick and brownstone façade topped with twin towers. The first renovation to the Colonial American–styled building added the Neo-Gothic narthex in 1887, enhanced with a

The Roland Pulpit at Zion German Evangelical Lutheran Church.

stained-glass window of *The Good Shepherd*. Look for the immigrant family in a bas-relief inscribed, "Remember the Lord in the Distant Land," a gift in 1955 from the City of Bremen.

Arts-and-crafts stenciled borders circle the walls in the rectangular nave, which holds six hundred members, while its balcony, faced with *The Luther Rose* (oak panels by Tyrolean woodcarvers), seats an additional four hundred. Eight stained-glass windows showing the life of Jesus were installed in 1891, along with the hand-carved eagle lectern, the altar niche and four windows of evangelists Matthew, Mark, Luke and John. The present oak pews, altar, pulpit and communion rail are from 1898, while the Leonardo da Vinci reproduction of *The Last Supper* belonged to the founding congregation.

Be sure to look up to the ceiling filled with Hoffman paintings from 1920 illustrating the petitions of the Lord's Prayer. Added at this time were the eight apostle windows from Munich on the balcony level: Philip with a cross-staff; Bartholomew with the flaying knife that took his life; James the Greater with hat, book and pilgrim's staff; Peter with the kingdom's keys; Paul with sword; Andrew with his X-shaped cross; Simon with a saw; and Thomas with his carpenter's square.

Also installed in the 1920s was the handsome Roland pulpit, faced with a three-dimensional oak carving of Roland of Bremen, an idealized knight from the Bugenhagen Bible. This edition of the Bible, translated by Martin Luther, was in Low German closer to the Dutch language and was suppressed by the government. Roland, who is said to have battled against the Moors in the kingdom of Hamburg, is depicted from an image found in the Cathedral of Bremen long before there was a united Germany.

Walnut bas-reliefs from 1923 frame each side of the altar: German composer J.S. Bach (1685–1750); prolific hymn writer Paul Gerhardt (1607–1676); and Martin Luther (1483–1546) and Philip Melanchthon (1497–1560), Christian reformers and founders of Lutheran doctrine. Luther's teachings, focusing on Christianity as taught in the Bible by prophets and apostles, are exemplified in this historic sanctuary, which fulfills the founding members' vision. The liturgy is still narrated in German, Christmas is traditionally celebrated with the crèche, representing the birth of Jesus, and *Willkommen* ("Welcome") on an exterior sign greets all visitors.

125 Henry Street, Brooklyn, NY 11201; 718-625-2276

BROOKLYN HEIGHTS SYNAGOGUE

With no Jewish house of worship existing in Brooklyn Heights, Rubin and Belle Huffman invited local families to their home on October 15, 1959, for an exploratory meeting to determine if there was enough interest in establishing a synagogue. Twenty people attended, and a committee was organized. While most were skeptical that a synagogue could survive, Huffman pushed on when one hundred people attended the second meeting, and with a great leap of faith, the members incorporated in January 1960. Since there was no money to purchase its own sanctuary, the group held the first High Holy Day service in September 1960 at First Unitarian Church, with more than five hundred people in attendance. Other neighboring churches—First Presbyterian, Spencer Mew Memorial, Holy Trinity and Grace Episcopal Church—also extended invitations to the fledgling synagogue to utilize their premises until it could finance a permanent home.

With great joy, members opened their first synagogue in 1974 in a Victorian brownstone from 1856 that once housed the Brooklyn Engineers Club at 117 Remsen Street; it is now the home of B'Nai Abraham, an orthodox congregation. Due to impressive growth that defied all the skeptics, the present sanctuary was acquired in 1995. The Greek Revival brownstone, built in 1858 as the Brooklyn Club, was a former meeting place for politicians and businessmen. The building lost its original exterior staircase, cornice and window frames, but it still has an original portico resting on gray limestone columns.

The interior of the modern sanctuary was skillfully designed using the building's fifty-foot width. A horizontal skylight adds a sense of serenity to this haven filled with pale wood-paneled walls and a sacred ark of honey-stained mahogany created by local Brooklyn artists Alex and Lorelei of Gruss Studios. Imbedded on the ark's façade is a tree of life in the shape of a menorah, while a dark metal menorah from the 1940s stands grandly against a cream-colored wall. An eternal light from the previous sanctuary now has an updated thin brass overhang shaped as the Shield of David.

PART I

Celebrating the joyous nine-day festival of Sukkot, a holiday of thanksgiving for the harvest, members build an outdoor hut (a sukkot) representing the temporary shelter of Israelites traveling in the Mount Sinai desert. While the sukkot is filled with fruits of the bounty, it is also a reminder of how this congregation fashioned a synagogue from temporary shelters and reaped its rewards.

131 Remsen Street (Henry and Clinton Streets), Brooklyn, NY 12201; 718-522-2070

OUR LADY OF LEBANON MARONITE CATHEDRAL

Round arches identify what is thought to be one of the first Romanesque Revival designs built in America, while artifacts purchased at an auction add unique touches to the landmark sanctuary. It was the Church of the Pilgrims before that congregation merged with Plymouth Church in 1934. Brooklyn Maronites, founded in 1902 in a Hicks Street brownstone, moved here in 1944 and were joined by members from St. Joseph's Church in Lower Manhattan. Rites were held in Syriac for the mostly Brooklyn Syrian group, which resided along Atlantic Avenue, but Arabic would be added for the Lebanese from Manhattan.

In 1890, the first Maronite church opened in Lower Manhattan and was replaced in 1947 with a new building, both under the patronage of St. Joseph. That structure was razed to build the World Trade Center, and the church's original cornerstone, uncovered at Ground Zero after September 11, 2001, is now displayed in the narthex.

This Eastern Rite Catholic group is named for Maro, a fourth-century Syrian monk who lived as a hermit on Cyrus Mountain and performed miraculous cures. His followers founded a sanctuary on the mountainside of Lebanon that remains the center of the Maronite

The Normandy Doors of Lebanon Maronite Cathedral.

Church. When the American group moved its seat, or eparchy, from Detroit in 1978, the bishop's presence soon recognized this sanctuary as a cathedral. Look for the patriarchal coat of arms, with a pair of cedar trees, above the center door. Cedars, a symbol of Lebanon, are considered sacred trees admired for their endurance and are exalted in the Old Testament (Ezekiel 31).

Architecture

In 1844, Richard Upjohn designed this massive gray stone structure with tower and spire, but the church was expanded in 1869 with a High Victorian addition by Leopold Eidlitz. Exterior bronze doors on the west and south portals were salvaged from the *Normandie*, a luxury French liner that caught fire under mysterious circumstances when docked at the West 49th Street Hudson River pier in February 1942. The ship was being refitted for World War II, and records note that there was one fatality and two hundred injured. The doors remain a fitting tribute to innocent victims of war. Look for roundels of the ocean liner *Isle de France*, Norman castles and six scenes of the French province of Normandy, including the Cathedral of St. Louis.

When you enter the narthex, note the salvaged mahogany doors from the Charles Schwab mansion, along with marble walls that once filled the Schwab dining room. The nave's three crystal chandeliers from Spain were installed in the 1950s and hang from a vaulted ceiling with a star-filled sky. In the baptistery, be sure to study the four-hundred-year-old European gates filled with imagery: St. Rocco with his wounded body and faithful dog at his side, distributing arms to the poor; a cardinal wearing a zucchetto (skull cap) and extending a blessing; and chubby putti (angels) carrying symbols of the cardinal's office: the orb, a globe and his wide-brimmed hat.

In 1961, painted glass windows, replacing Tiffany windows that had traveled with the former congregation to Plymouth Church, were created by two artisans. Jean Crotti of France designed the upper sections and the huge royal blue entrance window, and Saliba Douaihy of Lebanon created images of the apostles in the lower halves. Douaihy also produced the huge mural behind the main altar, featuring Our Lady of Harissa looking down the coastline from Lebanon's mountains.

113 Remsen Street (and Henry Street), Brooklyn, NY 11201; 718-624-7228

GRACE CHURCH

Many of the neighborhood's founding families—Pierrepont, Packer, Litchfield and Middagh—along with Trinity Church, financed this new building in 1847. Names of members are immortalized throughout the sanctuary, as well as on street signs. The site, tucked among private homes and cultivated gardens, was once part of the Remsen Farm, which overlooked New York Harbor. This Episcopal parish was started in 1841 as Emmanuel Church on Sidney Place, now the site of St. Charles Borromeo Church.

Richard Upjohn, Brooklyn native and prolific church architect, had just completed Trinity Church's third building in Manhattan, as well as Church of the Ascension on lower 5th Avenue. He designed this red and gray cast sandstone haven in the Gothic Revival style of the day, with a small tower at the corner of Hicks Street and Grace Court that held the clergy entrance.

Look up in the interior's rectangular nave to a carved black walnut ceiling and to the trefoil window tucked high above the chancel (altar area) for a portrait of a white-winged angel or perhaps a benefactor. Over the alabaster altar, three stained-glass panels by Lamb & Company articulate the psalm of thanksgiving, *Te Deum Laudamus* ("We Praise Thee, O God"), and feature four church dignitaries: the apostle Peter, with keys signifying his leadership of the Christian movement; the Old Testament king David, with harp and scepter; the first Christian martyr St. Stephen, with a palm leaf of martyrdom; and St. Augustine, bishop of Hippo, with mitre (hat) and crosier (staff), symbols of his office.

Be sure to see the three opalescent Tiffany windows, donated after 1880: Jesus with the sisters Mary and Martha; Madonna with child and two guardian angels; and the rendering of the Sermon on the Mount. Louis Comfort Tiffany (1848–1933) has many stained-glass works in Brooklyn's spiritual places, including pieces within family vaults at Green-Wood Cemetery (see entry), where both he and his father, Charles, are eternal guests. Tiffany's windows are far greater memorials than ornamental jewels, for it is in sanctuaries that his name will always be remembered.

254 Hicks Street (and Grace Court), Brooklyn, NY 11201; 718-624-1850

ST. CHARLES BORROMEO CHURCH

Reverend Charles Constantine Pise (1818–1868), who had been pastor of St. Peter's on Barclay Street in Manhattan and was the first Catholic chaplain to minister to the U.S. Senate in 1832, founded this Roman Catholic congregation in 1849. He purchased this site from Grace Episcopal Church (see entry), but fire destroyed the building; the cornerstone for the present church was dedicated the following year, in 1869.

Patron Charles (1538–1584) descended from the noble family of Borromeo in Italy and was granted his doctorate in civil and canon law at the University of Pavia in 1559. Pope Pius IV, elected to the papacy in 1559, was formerly Cardinal de Medici and also Charles's uncle. He appointed his nephew cardinal and archbishop of Milan at the age of twenty-two. While in Rome, Charles founded the Vatican Academy for literary study and served as papal secretary of state, being active in enforcing reforms from the Council of Trent in 1562. Charles became well known for his work during a devastating plague that swept Milan in 1575 and is shown above the altar in a vibrant window.

Designed by Patrick C. Keely, the red brick English Gothic sanctuary sits on Sidney Place, named for English author and statesman Sir Philip Sidney, who served at the sixteenth-century court of Queen Elizabeth. Look for the adjoining street named for Reverend Ambrose Aitken, a former pastor of the congregation.

The cruciform interior, with seating for 1,300, has a dark wood ceiling rising 130 feet and fourteen stained-glass windows from F.X. Zettler of the Royal Bavarian Art Institute. Cream-colored walls hold framed portraits of seven former pastors, while the vaulted ceiling features painted icons of Christianity, papal crests and images of the apostles. The focus of the apse is an ornately carved white marble reredos (altar screen) holding an oversized sculpture of the Crucifixion. Ten stained-glass images are set into the apse's wainscoting, attesting to the age of the sanctuary.

21 Sidney Place (between Henry and Clinton Streets), Brooklyn, NY 11201; 718-625-1177

THE ISLAMIC MISSION OF AMERICA
(DAWOOD MOSQUE)

This red brick row house, a four-story building tucked into a residential street and declared a landmark in 1966, was once a private home before being purchased by a member of the Islamic community in 1968. It became a Sunni mosque in 1977.

Members belong to the second-largest faith in the world, next to Christianity. Worldwide, more than 1.1 billion people practice the tenets and ceremonies of Islam, divided among two principal sects, the Sunni and the Shia. New York City claims an estimated 400,000 to 600,000 worshipers. The Sunni, representing about 84 percent of Moslems in the world, follow orthodox tradition and accept the four caliphs (heads of the Moslem state) as rightful successors to Muhammad. The Shia split from the Sunnis by rejecting this oral tradition and remain at odds over who shall lead the sect.

At the age of forty, Muhammad (570?–632), who was a wealthy merchant in Mecca, experienced a revelation. He believed himself to be called by Allah (God) to be the Arabian prophet of the true religion. Muhammad's life was filled with many revelations and visions, all of which are collected in the Quran, Islam's holy book, in which Old and New Testament prophets are also honored. Among them are Abraham, Isaac, Ishmael, David, Moses, John the Baptist and Jesus. Muhammad is said to be the last prophet, and his teachings include that mankind must submit to God's teachings, that heaven and hell await the present generation and that the world will end one day with a great judgment.

In this orthodox tradition, men and women worship separately. Women pray on the temple's upper floor, while men worship on the lower level. All visitors abide by Islamic custom and remove footwear before entering the prayer room. Since the religion forbids the use of figurative design, all motifs are represented in geometric patterns.

The mosque holds the minbar, the pulpit for the imam (who is the leader of the congregation), and the mihrab, a niche representing the presence of the prophet. It points toward Mecca, the Saudi Arabian birthplace of Muhammad that is the center of the Moslem world and where every Moslem aspires to visit on a pilgrimage (haj) at least once in his or her lifetime. This is to fulfill one of the five pillars of Islam. The others include the Declaration of Faith ("There is no God but God [Allah]"), almsgiving, fasting and prayer five times a day. Many who have journeyed to Mecca add the honorary title of Haj to their name.

143 State Street (off Bond Street), Brooklyn, NY 11201; 718-875-6607

Cobble Hill and Carroll Gardens

Cobble Hill, once part of Red Hook, was named for the steep hill on the road that intersects Court and Pacific Streets and Atlantic Avenue. The Dutch called it Ponkiesburg, and during the Battle of Long Island in the Revolutionary War, the hill functioned as a lookout post. The neighborhood quickly grew into a residential suburb after 1836 when ferry service began from Manhattan to Atlantic Avenue. The hill was removed, and by 1879, innovative Victorian-styled tenement buildings by Alfred White were filling with Irish, German and Scandinavian immigrants. After World War I, Middle Easterners from Lebanon and Syria arrived, followed by families from Puerto Rico. Cobble Hill, now a historic district, remains filled with many sacred havens.

Carroll Gardens, bordered by the Gowanus Canal, was also part of Red Hook. Its name was created by realtors in the 1960s and honors both an Irish signer of the Declaration of Independence (Charles Carroll from Maryland) and the Maryland Regiment from the Battle of Brooklyn (see the Stone House Museum in Park Slope). Today, the neighborhood's good housing stock is an asset, especially garden-fronted brownstones occupied by Italian descendants and families from original German and Irish settlers.

South Brooklyn was the official designation of Cobble Hill and Carroll Gardens when the city of Brooklyn was centered up north. Local residents still use the name while giving directions. South Brooklyn developed into distinct neighborhoods when expressways divided and destroyed its streets.

ST. PAUL'S ROMAN CATHOLIC CHURCH

St. Paul's Irish congregation was started in 1836 by Reverend John DuBois, pastor of St. Patrick's Cathedral on Mott Street in Manhattan. Two other congregations joined St. Paul's Church in 1970: St. Peter's, founded in 1859 on Hicks Street, and Our Lady of Pilar, begun in 1916 for the Hispanic community, which had merged with St. Peter's in the 1930s.

Irish immigrant Cornelius Heeney (1754–1848), founder of the Brooklyn Benevolent Society and always known for his kind spirit, donated the present site. Heeney told of being stranded, unable to pay for ferry passage until he met a Quaker, whose sect had been in Brooklyn when the Dutch ruled. Giving Heeney the one dollar he needed, the man told him, "Whenever thou seest a fellow creature in want of a dollar as thou art now, give it to him, and thou wilt have repaid me." The bachelor Heeney became a successful fur trader and left his fortune to the New York Orphan Asylum to care for and educate thousands of children. Look for his bas-relief portrait on a marble headstone in the church cemetery, where he is at perpetual rest.

As Brooklyn's second Roman Catholic church, the congregation chose as its patron Paul, who was the son of a Jew and a Roman citizen. Always known as a passionate man, Paul studied law and was violently opposed to Christian teaching. While on the road to Damascus, legend has it that Paul was struck blind and speechless by a flashing light. Look at the nave's stained glass for the dramatic story. Upon recovery, he converted to "The Way"—a phrase used before "Christian"—and celebrated in a local synagogue proclaiming Jesus to be the son of God. Paul's great legacy is his record of missionary adventures known as the Epistles and Acts of the Apostles, recorded in the New Testament. Since he became a defender of Christianity, Paul is usually portrayed with a sword.

Interior sanctuary of St. Paul Roman Catholic Church.

The red brick sanctuary, like its congregation, was merged into the haven seen today. Its original Greek Revival building, with columns flanking the entrance, was designed in 1835 by Gamaliel King, who planned Brooklyn's Borough Hall. In the 1860s, a central entry tower with Gothic façade was designed by Patrick C. Keely. In 1888, the exterior stucco veneer was applied, while low flanking stair towers and a new sanctuary were installed in 1906, thus completing the footprint of the present church.

Enter into a lobby faced with pink marble walls and a wide, red-carpeted staircase. A colorful rectangular interior, with deep teal touches on wood-faced fluted columns and balcony, pays tribute to Independence Hall in Philadelphia. Look up to see an elaborate Viennese ceiling said to be influenced by early pastor Joseph Schneller, who also imported stained-glass windows from Austria.

High above the chancel, an elaborately carved wooden screen is centered with the *Great Rood*, a depiction of the Crucifixion often found in old churches. On the marble reredos, Gothic niches are filled with angels and images of the four evangelists, while life-size marble statues of the apostles Peter and Paul stand freely on the altar platform. They are thought to be from the reredos replaced in 1928 or from St. Peter's Church. Reverend Mychal Judge, the New York City Fire Department chaplain who perished on September 11, 2001, was baptized and educated at St. Paul's and often returned to visit old friends. Stop by the Chapel of St. Elizabeth Seton, opened daily for meditation, and peek into the cemetery, which is located next door to the church office.

190 Court Street (and Congress Street), Brooklyn, NY 11201; 718-624-3425

COBBLE HILL PARK

Since this small public park (just 0.585 acre) was built on the site of the Second Unitarian Church around 1858, it remains an ideal spot to rest your spirit. The community protested the construction of a supermarket in the 1970s and was instrumental in opening this peaceful green haven, dedicated by Mayor Edward Koch in 1989.

Congress and Clinton Streets

KANE STREET SYNAGOGUE (BAITH ISRAEL ANSHEI EMES)

Founded in 1856, Kane Street is Brooklyn's oldest Conservative Jewish group and is fondly known as "Mother Synagogue." The congregation relocated to this site when its downtown sanctuary was demolished for the Brooklyn House of Detention. Today's brick and brownstone Romanesque Revival haven was built in 1855 for the Dutch Middle Reformed Church. Trinity German Lutheran Church had been in residence from 1857 until 1905, when the present congregation took possession of the building. The Sol and Lillian Goldman Center was constructed in 2004 to include social facilities and classrooms.

The portico's exterior archways, symmetrically placed below the brown stucco façade's stained-glass windows, lead into the sanctuary, while a small roofline spire distinguishes the temple from snuggly fitted private residences on Clinton Street. With seating for almost nine hundred, the interior is filled with colored glass windows, high vaulted ribbed ceiling and an original white wood balcony supported by thin columns. Sit on red velvet cushions lining white pews trimmed in mahogany and read biblical lessons in the windows: *Love Thy Neighbor as Thyself*, *Depart from Evil and Do Good* and *Seek Peace and Pursue It*.

The focus of the sanctuary, a bright white ark reflecting the building's Romanesque design, glows like an evening star against a wine-colored wall. Vivid stained-glass images of the Decalogue (Ten Commandments) are placed above the ark, while the bema (a table where the sacred Torah is read), has free-standing brass menorahs on either side. This nineteenth-century haven remains well cared for by twenty-first-century members.

236 Kane Street (between Court and Clinton Streets), Brooklyn, NY 11231; 718-875-1550

CHRIST CHURCH AND HOLY FAMILY

As a result of the city's rapidly growing population, the Episcopal Diocese opened its fourth Long Island church on this site in 1837. Land was donated by Nicholas Luquer, a parishioner whose name graces a local street, and in 1841, neighbor and architect Richard Upjohn designed and had constructed the English Gothic church. The stone exterior has a massive square bell

Christ Church.

tower with a crenellated roofline that tops off at 117 feet. After the tower was struck by lightning, resulting in the tragic death of neighbor Richard Schwartz, its four steeples were removed in August 2012. Note the red wood entrance doors symbolizing the blood of Christian martyrs, a matching tympanum displaying a three-dimensional polychrome image of the Crucifixion as a symbol of salvation and the iron fence with finials on its posts dating from 1861.

A former dark wooden interior with lofty ceiling was redesigned in 1917 through the generosity of three sisters, who engaged Louis Comfort Tiffany to modernize Upjohn's sanctuary. Balconies were removed, new windows were designed and the apse was renovated with a simple marble altar table. An inlayed reredos was adorned with the four-foot-square mother-of-pearl motif in the shape of Ezekiel's Wheel. It symbolizes four visions, as told in the book of the prophet Ezekiel, from the fall of Jerusalem to its restored theocracy.

Tiffany's marble work was expertly restored after fire ravaged the nave in 1939. Look in a dark walnut niche for his baptismal font with a gilded Gothic cover, as well as on the marble pulpit faced with Tiffany glass inlays. Several Tiffany windows survived the fire: young Jesus preaching to his elders in the temple; Lazarus being risen from the dead; and one of Tiffany's most popular images, the resurrection angel guarding the tomb of Jesus as three women approach the burial site. Several windows were damaged in the 2012 lightning storm, and members once again face restoration challenges.

This congregation opened Christ Chapel in 1867, near the Red Hook docks, for mission work among newly arriving immigrants. It is now Red Hook Pentacostal Holiness Church (see entry) and is still fulfilling its original purpose.

326 Clinton Street (and Kane Street), Brooklyn, NY 11231; 718-624-0083

SOUTH BROOKLYN SEVENTH-DAY ADVENTIST CHURCH

When Brooklyn was an independent city, this church was down south, hence the name. Seventh-Day Adventists celebrate their Sabbath on Saturday, which they count as the seventh day of creation, and focus on Bible studies. Archives reveal that the sect established the Brooklyn City Mission in 1886 and opened many churches throughout the borough.

The present sanctuary was built in 1905 by Theobald Engelhardt for Trinity German Lutheran Church, which had sold its previous site to the Kane Street Synagogue (see entry). The German members lived at a time when congregations had ethnic designations as part of their churches' official names. This Gothic brick church, with a double-curved arch over its bright blue doors, has lost the façade's stained glass that once filled corniced windows, but double lancets lining the interior's narrow sanctuary have retained their colorful glass panels.

249 DeGraw Street (between Clinton and Tompkins Place), Brooklyn, NY 11231

ST. AGNES ROMAN CATHOLIC CHURCH

The legend of the young patron Agnes is celebrated in eight stained-glass windows that tell her dramatic life story. She lived during the reign of Roman emperor Diocletian, who passed an edict in AD 303 against the practice of Christianity. Look for Agnes being thrown into raging flames, with fire engulfing onlookers but her body remaining untouched, for she would not give up her beliefs nor consent to marry a nobleman. The nave also displays her white marble image with a fern indicating martyrdom and a lamb for her innocence (Agnes was slain at the age of thirteen).

Reverend James Duffy started the parish in 1878 for the many Irish immigrants who overflowed from nearby St. Paul's and St. Mary Star of the Sea. Services were held in a private home until the congregation could build a wooden church. Today, the site holds its third building, a granite church dedicated in 1913 to replace a sanctuary destroyed by fire in 1901. This huge Neo-Gothic haven was designed by Thomas F. Houghton, who filled the stone exterior with enough spires and finials to tower over the neighborhood.

The cruciform interior has a marble reredos with elaborate tracery, Gothic finials and traditional bas-reliefs found in early twentieth-century sanctuaries. Look for Abraham, whose arm is restrained by a winged angel to stop the sacrifice of his son, Isaac, and also Melchizedek, the royal priest of ancient Jerusalem from whom all ordained priests trace their ministry.

The traditional rose window is faced with the Shield of David in limestone tracery and a colorful image of King David with his harp. Be sure to look up to the clerestory, filled with vivid stained glass and featuring apostles and patriarchs, while there are huge masterpieces of the Resurrection and the Nativity in the shallow transept. All windows are from the studio of Franz X. Zettler of the Royal Bavarian Art Institute in Munich, Germany, whose records and workshops were destroyed during World War II.

417 Sackett Street (and Hoyt Street), Brooklyn, NY 11231; 718-625-1717

ST. MARY STAR OF THE SEA
ROMAN CATHOLIC CHURCH

Records note that an Irish congregation founded the church in 1854 in the area of Red Hook now identified as Carroll Gardens. Since the sanctuary

Mourning, the World War I memorial in the garden at St. Mary Star of the Sea.

was near the docks, it was dedicated to Mary as patron of seafarers. Still on the original corner site purchased by Reverend Bacon, the present Gothic church was built by Patrick C. Keely in 1870, but fire ravaged the interior two years later. It was refurbished and continually supported by longshoremen and their families.

Beige stucco now covers a brick façade topped with a slate roof, while a squat bell tower holds its original clock. The building, well distanced from its gated street entrance, has a serene interior with seating for two thousand in decorative wooden pews. The nave, lined by Gothic arches and Corinthian columns adorned with gilded capitals, has glorious windows that tell the life story of Mary: as a young girl being presented in the temple by her mother, Ann; her betrothal to Joseph; and the birth of her son, Jesus. Brilliant gold mosaics highlight the fourteen Stations of the Cross portraying the death of Jesus.

Italian immigrants, who also toiled on the docks and established family businesses, would later settle in the parish and apply their well-honed artistic skills to restore icons and renew the sanctuary. Records show that Al Capone, infamous leader of Chicago gangsters, lived nearby and exchanged marriage vows at the church in 1918 with Mary May Coughlin. Red Hook was home to the Mafia in the 1920s, but Al was moving on to bigger projects.

Be sure to stop by the stark white statue *Mourning*, placed outside the rectory and dedicated to "St. Mary's boys who died in the World War." No year is indicated on the World War I memorial, for who could have imagined that there would be another conflict.

467 Court Street (between Nelson and Luquer Streets), Brooklyn, NY 11231; 718-625-2270

SANTA MARIA ADDOLORATA

This large shrine is identified as the patron saint of Vola di Bari. Located in a well-tended private garden, the statue represents an important Italian tradition of bringing the town's Madonna to the New World for protection and good fortune. Look for the Court Street shrine between 3rd and 4th Streets.

ST. STEPHEN ROMAN CATHOLIC CHURCH AND SACRED HEART OF JESUS AND MARY

When the BQE slashed through the neighborhood, it just missed St. Stephen's, founded in 1866 by Irish immigrants. Not so lucky was Sacred Heart Church, founded in 1882 as an Italian-speaking parish on Hicks Street, which was demolished to make way for the Brooklyn Battery Tunnel. Both congregations merged in 1941 within this huge red brick Neo-Gothic church designed by Patrick C. Keely.

Relevant Italian Madonnas and saints line side aisles filled with colorful figurative stained-glass windows. Keely's archives record that many were produced by Morgan Brothers. Mother Frances Cabrini arrived in 1892 to open the Sacred Heart parish school, and the community never forgot her dedication to their ancestors. The public mural unveiled in June 2012 at 500 Hicks Street honors Mother Cabrini's legacy, as well as the work of Italian American women. The bridge near the church allows the community to cross over the BQE at noisy Hicks Street.

108 Carroll Street (Summit and Hicks Streets), Brooklyn, NY 11231; 718-596-7750

St. Paul's Episcopal Church of Brooklyn

An Irish congregation of successful South Brooklyn businessmen was organized in 1849 when the town was called Brooklyn. The designation remains part of its official name because another St. Paul's Episcopal Church was organized in 1836 in the town of Flatbush. Members, who traveled daily to Manhattan by ferry, first built a wooden church on Carroll Street near the harbor.

Meanwhile, the Oxford movement (1833–45) had taken place in England and spread to America. Reverend John Keble urged the Anglican Church to return to its Catholic roots, but because of anti-Catholic prejudices, Keble's efforts to revive rituals caused heated controversy.

By 1890, St. Paul's members were relocating to greener pastures, while Italian, Norwegian and Middle Eastern immigrants were moving into recently built apartment houses and working on the waterfront. In 1907, the church was ravaged by fire, but a decision was made to refurbish the building and adopt Anglo-Catholic rituals. A new rector, Andrew Chalmers Wilson, reached out to immigrants and revitalized the sanctuary with the Oxford movement's recommended form of worship. Between 1928 and 1934, West Indian immigrants arrived, making the congregation as diverse as Brooklyn itself.

In 1987, another fire destroyed pews and clerestory windows and damaged the front of the nave. Again, the congregation skillfully restored the building and continued to care for priceless artifacts in its historic sanctuary. Restored wall stencils attest to their labor of love.

Architecture

Pulpit of St. Paul's Episcopal Church of Brooklyn.

Richard M. Upjohn, son of the church architect and partner in the family firm, was a member of the congregation when asked to take this project. He designed a High Victorian Gothic stone exterior with sandstone trim, a tower rising 185 feet and three sandstone arches that define the front porch. The sanctuary was constructed from 1866 to 1884, with an interior nave that seats one thousand worshipers and a polychrome hammer-beam ceiling that rises 60 feet.

The fire in 1907 destroyed most of the interior, but original black walnut pews and matching wainscoting survived. Brownstone columns still stand on massive pedestals, and Upjohn's elaborate stone capitals remain filled with nineteenth-century carvings. The bearded man with a triangle is said to be the architect himself.

Original nonfigurative stained-glass windows are from Upjohn's design, as is the traditional rose window. Look above the high altar for ten more of the architect's English glass designs. Life-size marble statues of Peter as bishop and Paul with his sword as defender of Christianity were from Italy in 1913 and frame the apse's seven sanctuary lamps.

After the 1907 fire, Neo-Gothic architect Ralph Adams Cram, known for his attention to detail and polychrome technique, was asked to redesign the sanctuary. He cleverly placed his carved pulpit, whose wood façade holds eight images of teachers and writers, halfway down the nave for all to hear the sermons. In 1910, Cram designed the intimate Lady Chapel, with a serene white marble altar placed against dark wainscoting. Tucked into the far right side of the chancel is St. Joseph's Chapel, featuring Joseph the Carpenter; St. Anne, his mother-in-law; and Joseph of Arimathea, a rabbi who offered his tomb to bury Jesus before sundown. Ten smaller figures include Edward Pusey, who revived the controversial Anglo-Catholic liturgy.

An intricate background and exquisite colors are found on all of Cram's altars, including the St. Anthony of Padua altar from 1917. Anthony has five of the Franciscan followers on the façade, among them Clare, who founded an order of sisters, and Juniper Serro, who founded the California missions in America. Cram planned the St. Francis altar as a tribute to chaplains who ministered to armed forces in the trenches. Golden fleur-de-lis (lilies) on a sky blue background are reminders of soldiers dying on French fields in World War I (1914–18).

To welcome all visitors, the congregation wrote a self-guided tour, filled with names and places that recall a time when St. Paul's ministered to a wealthier class and before highways divided the neighborhood and doctrine divided the congregation.

199 Carroll Street (and Clinton Street), Brooklyn, NY 11231; 718-625-4126

CHURCH OF JESUS CHRIST OF LATTER-DAY SAINTS

This sect, whose modern white brick building was formerly the Longshoremen's Union Hall, moved to the present location in 1994 and is admired for a firm dedication to family life. Officially organized in 1830 in Fayette, New York, as the Church of Christ, Mormon congregations are led by a lay priesthood that is not a distinct class within their church. Every worthy man can become a priest at the age of sixteen. While women cannot become priests, they can preach and give sermons, teach Sunday school and run youth organizations. Mormons practice the ordinances of Baptism, Confirmation, Matrimony, Holy Eucharist and Holy Orders and enlist for two years in missionary service.

PART I

Records note that Mormons were in Brooklyn from 1837, but there is no written history until 1898, when the Church of Brooklyn was recognized in official meeting minutes. The Brooklyn Chapel was opened in 1918 on Gates and Franklin Avenue and would be the first sanctuary built east of the Mississippi since the Mormons were driven out of New York in 1846. It would grow into an independent branch and play host to developing congregations. The branch would divide many times, forming a Spanish branch in 1978 and a Chinese branch in 1979.

This chapel, known as the Park Slope Branch, grew out of the Midwood Chapel. Its serene sanctuary is filled with light wood pews, a center pulpit and a side table used for the ordinance of the Eucharist. Mormons have no icon to represent Jesus nor any adornments in the chapel, but music accompanies the members' choir during services. While nonmembers are invited into the chapel, only Mormons can enter into the temple sanctuary.

Other than the Bible, members read three books of scripture, including the Book of Mormon, named for ancient American prophets and which contains an eyewitness account of Jesus on the American continent after his resurrection in Jerusalem. It was translated from golden plates discovered and published in 1830 by the group's founder and prophet, Joseph Smith (1805–1844) of Palmyra, New York, who experienced his vision in 1820. Smith was told to restore the original church organized by Jesus Christ, but he would eventually be murdered, and his followers were driven out of the state.

In 1846, a church group from Illinois led by Brigham Young began traveling across the Great Plains to Salt Lake Valley, while a New York group chartered the ship *Brooklyn* and sailed with 224 members from Old Slip in Lower Manhattan to California. A plaque to mark the twenty-thousand-mile religious exodus of Mormons to the West has been placed at Old Slip.

No longer thinking that all followers would come to Salt Lake City in Utah, Mormons are altering tradition and opening neighborhood chapels, but thanks must be given to the sect for its genealogical research that is available to trace ethnic roots and connect with family members, a basic tenet of Mormon life.

343 Court Street (and Union Street), Brooklyn, NY 11231; 718-237-8859

Fort Greene and Boerum Hill

Fort Greene, named for Revolutionary War general Nathanael Greene, was said to have held the largest regiment on Long Island during the 1776 Battle of Long Island. It was rebuilt again for the War of 1812. The historic area is bordered on the east by the Brooklyn Navy Yard, in operation from 1801 to 1966 and now buzzing with industry. The neighborhood also includes the Brooklyn Academy of Music, a performing arts center founded in 1861 that relocated to its new building by Herts and Tallant in 1908. Ambitious restoration plans, which added an undulating exterior canopy by Hugh Hardy as a twenty-first-century safeguard from storms, have revitalized the academy.

Fort Greene Park, originally Washington Park, was the military site that was assigned as Brooklyn's first park in 1847 through the efforts of Walt Whitman, who thought that this overpopulated area needed recreational space. The thirty-acre site was redesigned in 1867 by Frederick Law Olmsted and Calvert Vaux of Central Park fame, while the Raymond Ingersoll and Walt Whitman Houses—which were completed in 1944 as the largest public housing project, with 3,500 apartments on thirty-eight acres—face one of the park's borders.

Boerum Hill, commonly called South Brooklyn, is filled with charming three-story row houses first built for working-class New Yorkers. In the 1900s, when masses of immigrants started to arrive, these homes were divided into apartments, but gentrification has restored most low-rise residences to one-family status. The original area was farmland belonging to the eighteenth-century Boerum family, who were involved in colonial government. There are more than twenty-nine sacred havens in both neighborhoods that have witnessed every immigrant group passing through Brooklyn.

Atlantic Avenue, south of downtown Brooklyn, is a major thoroughfare that was once known for its cluster of Middle Eastern businesses and restaurants. While it's a short walk from Fort Greene to busy Fulton Mall, Atlantic Avenue runs through many neighborhoods, including Boerum Hill, Cobble Hill, Prospect Heights, Crown Heights, East New York and New Lots. The former Williamsburgh Savings Bank, with its enormous four-clock tower on the corner of Flatbush Avenue, is to date Brooklyn's only landmark skyscraper, topping off at 512 feet. A massive development over the Metropolitan Transit Authority (MTA) railyard now includes the Barclays sports arena, residential buildings and a shopping mall, all of which have transformed the neighborhood. Many Middle Eastern immigrants who first lived in this area, known as "Little Arabia," opened Arab havens for the Christian Rite and mosques that call Moslems to prayer five times a day.

St. Nicholas Antiochian Orthodox Cathedral

Father Raphael Hawaweeny (1860–1915), who founded the church in Lower Manhattan in 1895, guided Arabic Christian immigrants to Brooklyn's larger Arabic-speaking community in 1902. The congregation first rented a church on Pacific Street and made its final move in 1920 to the present site, which was built in 1857 as St. Peter's Episcopal Church.

Located in the middle of a residential street, the Gothic gray stone church that seats six hundred has its huge rose window of *Christ Pantocrator* (*Great High Priest*) outlined in limestone and accompanied by stained-glass lancets. Colorful mosaics enhance the tympana over each of three doors. Look for Patron Nicholas gracefully gazing on visitors and also see him remembered as "the wonder worker" on a golden icon in the nave. He was bishop of Myra (now called Dembre in Turkey) and died in about AD 350. He remains popular in both eastern and western Christianity as the original Santa Claus.

Walk into this dazzling church filled with artifacts, murals and crystal chandeliers and study the elaborate marble iconostatis adorned with more than two dozen gilded icons. It is topped by the *Holy Rood* (carved images of the Crucifixion), a vestige from St. Peter's congregation. Fluted wooden columns, original painted pews and the high pulpit demonstrate how the congregation worked within the former church's footprint to transform the

Interior of St. Nicholas Antiochian Orthodox Cathedral.

cream-colored interior for Orthodox rituals. Look up to the gallery that seats the liturgical choir, "the soul of the church" that chants Byzantine and Slavic prayers in English and Arabic. Colorful icons line the loft's façade, while an adorned ribbed ceiling is pierced by small Gothic windows.

This Orthodox church belongs to a universal group of about fourteen autocephalous (self-ruling) churches, each headed by a patriarch or archbishop and divided into geographical districts. But the tenets of their faith are identical and have been celebrated since the first century. The Antiochian North American group is part of the Patriarchate of Antioch in Damascus, Syria. It was in Antioch where the disciples of Jesus were first called Christians. Since St. Nicholas is the first and oldest parish in North America, it is the Mother Church and seat of the metropolitan archbishop. Look for the interior icon of St. Raphael Hawaweeny, the founding priest of the Syrian Mission who was canonized in 2000; he is also remembered with an exterior mosaic over the entrance.

55 State Street (between Hoyt and Bond Streets), Brooklyn, NY 11217; 718-855-6225

PART I

THE BAPTIST TEMPLE

Founded in 1823 during a yellow fever epidemic, this historic landmark is the fourth home of Brooklyn's first Baptist congregation. Elijah Lewis Jr. and Eliakim Raymond rowed from Manhattan and began their ministry by baptizing converts in the East River at the foot of Old Fulton Street.

Today, the congregation belongs to the Conservative Baptist Association. It baptizes only adults, strongly supports separation of church and state and believes that the Bible is the word of God. Since each church is run autonomously with no hierarchy, there was an enormous growth of Baptist churches throughout Brooklyn. They number over 150, with many found in a single neighborhood.

In 1917, the original temple from 1895 was destroyed by fire but was quickly rebuilt on the same site within the year. Services continue today in the Romanesque Revival sanctuary designed by Dodge & Morrison. The red brick building with brownstone details is anchored by a huge tower on its corner site, while round-arch windows dominate the façades of two street-level entrances. The J.W. Steere organ, with more than 2,500 golden pipes, has always been the temple's treasure, and it was lovingly restored by New York City native Keith Bigger, a member of the Organ Historical Society who attended this church with his parents.

The interior's high-arched white ceiling is filled with ribs and cornices that complement the dark woodwork surrounding lower walls. The chancel's opalescent stained-glass windows from the Brooklyn Art Glass Company portray Jesus in the city of Jerusalem, with apostles Peter on the Sea of Galilee and John in Nazareth. Since baptism is always by total immersion, the chancel's pool, tucked within oak doors, becomes the focus of the interior when its doors are opened. It remains in its original spot since the first church was built, and one can easily imagine earlier ceremonies in the East River.

360 Schermerhorn Street (and 3rd Avenue), Brooklyn, NY 11217; 718-875-1858

HOUSE OF THE LORD

The Swedish Pilgrim's Evangelical Church built this Romanesque Revival sanctuary in 1893 with enough space for social and cultural events. Its brick exterior has two banded-brick arched portals whose deep red doors signify Christian martyrdom. When entering the nave, look for the baptismal font with a golden image of the Holy Spirit in the form of a dove, reminding visitors that baptism is the entry into Christian life. Cream walls and dark wood wainscoting add serenity to the shallow auditorium that is surrounded by a gallery and softly tinted windows.

Moving here in the 1950s, this Pentecostal congregation was organized in 1929 by Reverend Alonzo A. Daughtry in Georgia, who wanted worship centered around Jesus and not a minister's charisma. The movement opened branches in Harlem and Brooklyn, and in 1958, the founder's son, Reverend Herbert Daughtry, continued his father's dream by becoming pastor and following the church motto, "Be ye not hearers of the word only, but doers also." Along with the congregation, Daughtry remains an activist for African American and neighborhood causes and has been honored for humanitarian service by the United States Congress.

415 Atlantic Avenue, Brooklyn, NY 11217; 718-596-1991

By the Way

St. Cyril's of Turau Orthodox Cathedral was founded in 1950 under the official title Belarussian Autocephalous Orthodox Church by immigrants from Belarus in the former Soviet Union, and it is the seat of the archbishop. Although the roof is topped by the triple bar Eastern Orthodox cross, a quatrefoil (ornament with four lobes) on the exterior's upper portion indicates that the corner church was built by a western Christian group. The red brick Gothic building from 1902 was formerly the Second United Presbyterian Church, and records indicate that in 1850 the property was owned by St. Peter's Episcopal Church. Three lancet windows dominate the unadorned cream-painted façade, while original wood entrance doors are approached through a recessed garden surrounded by an original black iron fence.

401 Atlantic Avenue (and Bond Street), Brooklyn, NY 11217; 718-875-0595

Templo Cristiano de Brooklyn (Brooklyn Christian Temple) is housed on the street level of a residential three-story brick building. The Gothic archway is flanked by small arched windows and features a white cross on the tympanum, while its bilingual name is displayed on a sandstone triangle over the entrance. An intimate rectangular interior focuses on a raised platform for the preacher, while pews line a narrow aisle. The use of former commercial space for religious chapels is found in many areas that cater to small ethnic congregations.

393 Atlantic Avenue (and Bond Street), Brooklyn, NY 11217

TWO MOSQUES

Masjid al-Farooq, located in a six-story Beaux-Arts former office building, is home to a Sunni Islamic group. Islam, a word meaning "peace," is based on the teachings of Muhammad, who believed in and taught of one God, Allah. This sanctuary became infamous in 1995 when its Egyptian imam, Sheik Omar Abdel Rashman, was convicted of plotting bombings in New York City. Sunni mosques are the most prevalent in New York City and are often located in easily accessed areas for daily prayer.

552 Atlantic Avenue (between 3ʳᵈ and 4ᵗʰ Avenues), Brooklyn, NY 11217; 718-875-6607

The Islamic Guidance Center, with the Ahlul Bayt Islamic Library, is a two-story Shiite mosque located directly across the street from the Sunni mosque. This brick haven with stucco façade was built in 1855 for the Atlantic Street Baptists, who relocated to Hanson Place (see entry). In 1860, St. Matthew's English Lutheran congregation resided here for almost twenty years, followed by the Metropolitan Mission, the Swedish Baptist Church in 1900, the Salvation Army in 1929 and the Brooklyn Tabernacle in 1970.

The ancient split from the Sunnis was caused by Shiites' rejection of the oral tradition of the four caliphs (heads of the Moslem state) as rightful successors to Muhammad. They represent about 20 percent of Moslems worldwide and are led by an ayatollah or mullah. Shiites mourn the Sunnis' slaying of Imam Hussein, Muhammad's grandson, and commemorate the deed annually. Using a prayer stone when they pray, Shiites bear a mark on their foreheads from hitting the stone.

543 Atlantic Avenue (between 3ʳᵈ and 4ᵗʰ Avenues), Brooklyn, NY 11217; 718-583-1390

THE PRISON SHIP MARTYRS' MONUMENT

The world's tallest Doric column, measuring over 148 feet and crowned with a lantern that was to hold an eternal light, stands solemnly on a plaza within Fort Greene Park. It honors at least 11,500 patriots who were imprisoned during the American Revolutionary War on eleven British ships standing off the coast of the Navy Yard in Wallabout Bay. Captured soldiers were left to die from starvation, overcrowding and disease, and the deceased were thrown overboard or buried along the shore. By 1873, twenty boxes filled with bones washed up on the shore had been placed in a vault now on the present site. By 1907, a committee had begun raising funds to erect this reminder of man's inhumanity to man. Although the Brooklyn-born poet Walt Whitman died before this memorial was planned, he left his thoughts in "The Wallabout Martyrs":

> *Greater than memory of Achilles or Ulysses,*
> *More, more by far to thee than tomb of Alexander,*
> *Those cart loads of old charnel ashes. Scales and splints of mouldy bones,*
> *Once living men—once resolute courage, aspiration, strength,*
> *The stepping stones to thee to-day and here, America.*

The marble sculpture by A.A. Weinman and plaza design by Stanford White were also adorned by a majestic bronze eagle stationed at each corner. Vandalism necessitated their removal, but the eagles landed again in 2008 on their original pedestals thanks to the New York City Parks Department. Stop by the Visitors' Center, also designed by White, for additional information.

From DeKalb Avenue to Myrtle Avenue and from Washington Street to St. Edwards Street.

LAFAYETTE AVENUE PRESBYTERIAN CHURCH

Founded in 1857 by staunch abolitionists, this congregation continues to combat social injustice as its birthright. Reverend Theodore Ledyard Cuyler (1822–1909), a friend of Abraham Lincoln, served as the first pastor and hosted meetings for the Brooklyn abolition movement. Lincoln's eldest son, Robert Todd, broke ground in 1860 for this Early Romanesque Revival brownstone building designed by Grimshaw and Morrill, with an oval interior that seats more than two thousand. Windows were later filled with figurative

Lafayette Presbyterian Church.

designs by renowned glass artists, even though Reverend Cuyler was not enamored of art glass. The pastor is fondly remembered as a neighborhood activist in Cuyler Gore Park, a triangle at Fulton Street.

Poet Marianne Moore (1887–1972), whose brother and grandfather were ministers and whose published work reflects the family's moral upbringing, was an active parishioner. When the church fell victim to the Independent Subway System (IND) construction in 1932 and lost its two-hundred-foot steeple, Moore wrote her poem "The Steeple Jack" to comfort the members.

Look up to the interior gallery for Tiffany windows of *Creation*, flanked by *Law* and *Gospel*. Pastor Cuyler is said to be the model for St. Paul preaching on Mars Hill. Be sure to see the only Tiffany window under the balcony, *The Consecration of Samuel by His Mother* from 1899, donated by Reverend Cuyler in his mother's memory, while four other Tiffany works, dating from 1893 to 1895, are placed on the clerestory level. In the Underwood Chapel, *Miracle of Creation*, installed in 1920 to remember Julia and Charles Wallerhand, is known as the Tiffany Company's final design. The sanctuary's other stained-glass pieces are attributed to Alex Locke of Arnold & Locke from Brooklyn, as well as Benjamin Sellers and Joseph Lauber of Manhattan.

Contemporary murals from 1976, together called *Great Cloud of Witnesses*, joyfully fill the clerestory's cream-colored walls. Artist Henry Prussing surprises visitors with life-size images of Brooklyn neighbors actively moving among traditional stained glass. His work reflects the church's motto, "A Church with an Historic Past Serving the Present Day," and is a reminder that the city is only its people.

85 South Oxford Street, Brooklyn, NY 11217; 718-625-7515

HANSON PLACE SEVENTH-DAY ADVENTIST CHURCH

This Greek Revival landmark building with Italianate details was designed in 1860 by George Penchard for the Hanson Place Baptists, whose members had been known as the Atlantic Street Baptists founded in 1857. It was common practice to rename congregations for new locations.

Hanson Place Seventh-Day Adventist.

In 1963, this sanctuary was acquired by the present group, which celebrates its Sabbath on Saturday. Bible school also meets on the Sabbath, dating from the tradition of a Bible school that Ludwig Hacker first organized in 1739 for German immigrants in Ephrata, Pennsylvania.

Cream-colored Corinthian pillars, corner windows and pediments enhance the red brick façade. Look for the congregation's name and the building's dedication date in stained glass over the main door of the tripartite entrance. Pale wood pews with a surrounding balcony add to the openness of the wine-carpeted nave, while Italianate windows flood the unadorned interior with light. The minister's pulpit is the focus of this Christian haven, which was skillfully restored in 1970 and remains a grand presence in the neighborhood.

88 Hanson Place (and South Portland Avenue), Brooklyn, NY 11217; 718-789-3030

HANSON PLACE CENTRAL METHODIST CHURCH

The sanctuary's cubelike exterior, designed in 1930 by Herts and Tallant of Brooklyn Academy of Music fame, is filled with Gothic arches, terra-cotta trimmings and two impressive entrances. It also has unusual exterior space occupied by retail stores, an income-producing idea that was planned by the foresighted congregation founded in 1847. This massive beige brick church, which had replaced a smaller church on this site, is dwarfed by the Williamsburg Bank Tower next door, but the sanctuary has kept its dignity while witnessing the neighborhood's transformation into a sports arena complex in 2012. This idea was proposed in 2003 by developer Bruce Ratner, who also developed the downtown MetroTech Center.

The first Methodist society was organized in Manhattan in 1766 by Irish lay preacher Philip Embury, a follower of the Anglican reformers. Embury's church is still standing in the financial district on John Street and was a division of the Church of England until after the American Revolution. In the spirit of democracy, the Methodist Church became an American entity.

144 St. Felix Street (Hanson Place), Brooklyn, NY 11217; 718-638-7360

EGLISE BAPTISTE FRANÇAISE

If the walls could talk, stories would be heard here in many languages. The sanctuary, built in 1870 as Simpson Methodist Church, was once the Jewish Center of Fort Greene. Presently, a Haitian Baptist congregation holds French services in this Italian Romanesque haven that is anchored by an exterior tower. The Shield of David remains engraved over the entryway, but it is now covered with the name of the new congregation. Look for alpha and omega symbols over the entry, as well as icons representing the Bible and the Ten Commandments in small roundels within tall, golden-colored glass windows.

209 Clermont Avenue (Willoughby Avenue), Brooklyn, NY 11217

THE PAUL ROBESON THEATER

This landmark church building, originally built in the 1860s for the Universalist Society, is a variation of the Romanesque Revival style and is thought to have been designed by Rembrandt Lockwood. It was purchased for a synagogue in 1870 by Temple Israel and again in 1890 by a Roman Catholic Polish group that placed it under the patronage of St. Casimir. The members added the exterior steeple and the interior apse, as well as stained-glass windows and murals. In 1980, St. Casimir's merged with Our Lady of Czenstochowa (see Sunset Park), and the sanctuary became home for a troupe of players. Dr. Josephine English purchased the haven in 1980 to establish an arts center for the community.

The brownstone space is a tribute to Paul Robeson (1898–1976), who was a masterful singer and actor and part of the Harlem Renaissance, a literary and artistic movement that drew black artists to New York City between 1925 and 1929. Look up to the interior's cream-colored vaulted ceiling, still displaying painted icons of the four evangelists who were the New Testament's storytellers, and to stained-glass windows left by the Polish congregation. See Theresa, the Carmelite nun, scattering red roses, seemingly for the actors on stage, while a winged angel holds an hourglass as a reminder of the importance of time.

40 Greene Avenue (between Carlton and Adelphi Street), Brooklyn, NY 11217

BETHLEHEM LUTHERAN CHURCH

Swedish Evangelical Lutherans, who built this light brick Romanesque church in 1894, engraved their name on a pink marble tympanum over the main entry and included the six-pointed Byzantine star as a good omen. Huge stained-glass windows over two entrances are enhanced by unusual verdigris copper frames with matching tracery. Look for the icon of an open book, which affirms Lutheran belief in scripture alone.

Early Swedish immigrants settled in Manhattan, and later arrivals worked at Brooklyn shipyards. They built small Lutheran churches, but since most of them have been demolished, Swedish footprints are almost wiped out of neighborhoods' history.

The Lutheran movement began in Germany, spread throughout Europe and came to America with the Dutch traders. During Martin Luther's Reformation, King Gustav II Adolf (1594–1632) of Sweden fought and died as a champion of Protestantism in the Thirty Years' War. Early Swedish immigrants brought their own style of Lutheran worship to the New World but were united in 1742 by Reverend Henry Melchior Muhlenberg (1711–1787), who formed the first North American synod and adopted a common liturgy. The pastor also kept detailed journals and left an impressive record of colonial life. It is interesting to note that the intolerant Dutch returned a Lutheran pastor to the Netherlands in 1657, but when Governor Peter Stuyvesant was forced to retire in 1664, Lutherans worshiped more freely under British rule. Swedish immigrants who founded this church left a sanctuary now rooted in a more tolerant Brooklyn.

490 Pacific Avenue (and 3rd Avenue), Brooklyn, NY 11217; 718-624-0242

Clinton Hill

W hen rural farmland was divided in 1832, Clinton Avenue became the fashionable suburban road for middle-class residents. It was named for New York mayor and governor (as well as sponsor of the Eire Canal) DeWitt Clinton (1769–1828). Since the neighborhood was far removed from the city, a wealthier class saw its potential, and in 1874, oil magnate Charles Pratt (1830–1891), a pioneer of the petroleum business, built his mansion on the avenue along with four homes for his children. His huge landholdings now belong to Pratt Institute, the visual art school that he endowed in 1887. Pratt was a self-made man without a college education, but he understood that higher learning would benefit the working class. Clinton Hill's fluid perimeter surrounds Fort Greene, Prospect Heights and Williamsburg, and its historic district has preserved mansions and churches built before the 1940s invasion of apartment buildings.

St. Mary's Episcopal Church

The long garden in front of the parish house extends a quiet welcome in the Pratt Institute neighborhood, while the landmark church projects the image of an English country chapel. The rural congregation, founded in 1836, held services in parishioners' homes and commissioned the firm of Renwick & Auchmuty to design this Gothic Revival church in 1858 on land that held an old schoolhouse. Its copper-topped tower, protruding bay and Gothic

St. Mary's Episcopal Church.

arch leading to a narrow lane add charm to its corner site on streets lined with distinctive buildings.

The interior's figurative stained-glass windows installed in the 1860s were patterned on early English designs,while Tiffany opaque glass work (including a fully armored St. George, patron of England) were later additions. Look in an English window for the inscription, "Never Turn Thy Face from Any Poor Man." An intimate apse with wood wainscoting surrounding the altar focuses on three glorious windows: Jesus, as the Good Shepherd cradling his sheep, and the Nativity and Annunciation, both in honor of the patron.

Slim wooden columns that support arcades beneath the dark oak-timber ceiling display Episcopal banners, as well as national flags from the present congregation. Ghana, Said, Cuba and the Dominican Republic are among several dozen represented. In 1996, a hand-crafted columbarium (vault for receiving ashes of the dead) was added by members, who have managed to retain their countrylike sanctuary within a booming borough.

230 Classon Avenue (and Willoughby Avenue), Brooklyn, NY 11205; 718-638-2090

St. Luke's Lutheran Church

In 1869, a German group that was weary of the Sunday ferry ride to Manhattan began worshiping in a rented church on Carlton Avenue. Twenty-five years later, when it was destroyed by fire, German-born Charles Pfizer (1824–1906), a member who was successful in the molasses business, purchased land from the Pratt family to build this Neo-Gothic stone church designed by J.W. Walter. By 1894, when the church was dedicated, the congregation included many wealthy industrialists. Charles Pfizer, who founded his company with his cousin, Charles Ehrhardt (1821–1891), retired from business, leaving his son to manage the firm that would evolve into an international pharmaceutical company; he dedicated more time to the new church building.

Upon entering the sanctuary, look in the cream-colored narthex for five colorful lancet windows of Old Testament prophets with German dedications: Moses, displaying the Ten Commandments; Isaiah with his scrolls; Ezekiel; Jeremiah; and Daniel.

A dark wooden altar enhanced by a carving of *The Last Supper* on the reredos is the focus of the high-vaulted sanctuary, while the apse is filled with wood wainscoting and a handsome carved pulpit. In the shallow transept, there is a huge window featuring three men who made Lutheran history: Martin Luther, founder of the Reformation movement that swept Roman Catholic Europe; Philip Melanchthon, who wrote the Augsburg Confession in 1530 to explain Luther's theses to King Charles V; and Johannes Bugenhagen, who organized the reformation within Germany and Scandinavia. Two angels flanking the German personalities complete the five-paneled work of art. Most windows are attributed to John La Farge and Louis Comfort Tiffany and are filled with references to the Bible, on which Luther's teachings are based. See *The Sermon on the Mount*, the memorial window for Pfizer, and *The Ascending Saviour*, the window remembering his partner Ehrhardt. German was utilized in services until 1905, when the next generation transitioned to English.

259 Washington Street (between Willoughby and DeKalb Avenues), Brooklyn, NY 11205; 718-622-5612

OUR LADY QUEEN OF ALL SAINTS CHURCH

The Roman Catholic church's forerunner, St. John's Chapel, which cared for a small congregation of European immigrants, was established in 1878 on the former site of Bishop John Loughlin's planned cathedral (see Downtown Brooklyn). During 1909, additional land was purchased from the Samuel Vernon estate to build this new sanctuary for Clinton Hill's growing population. The pastor of St. John's Chapel, Auxiliary Bishop George Mundelein, who would become the first cardinal of Chicago, creatively planned this large complex to include a school that would seamlessly surround the front of the French Gothic sanctuary.

Designed in 1910 by Gustave Steinback, the church pays homage to the thirteenth-century Sainte Chapelle, built in Paris by Louis IX. On the white

Our Lady Queen of All Saints.

stone façade, twenty-four saintly images by sculptor Joseph Sibbel adorn the entire midsection of the building, while medieval gargoyles and floating angels guard the rooftop. An elaborate portal holds a wheel window with stone tracery and features the monogram of Patron Mary.

Enter by a dramatic staircase within the narthex into a long, narrow stone interior with fourteen stained-glass figurative windows by Alex Locke and James M. Hughes; they tell biblical stories from the creation of man to the formation of the Christian church. Multitudes of images are reminders of early medieval churches that taught their histories through visual narratives. Soaring marble columns and graceful arches add to the sanctuary's serenity, while the baptismal font is placed at the nave's entrance as a reminder that baptism is the entry into Christian life. An elaborate reredos filled with spires, niches and six angels is surrounded by two huge tapestries that are pictorial tributes to the patron of this opulent church.

300 Vanderbilt Avenue (and Lafayette Avenue), Brooklyn, NY 11205; 718-638-7625

CADMAN MEMORIAL CONGREGATIONAL CHURCH

In 1943, Clinton Avenue Congregational Church merged with Clinton Avenue Community Church and named its new sanctuary in memory of Reverend S. Parkes Cadman (1864–1936). Downtown Cadman Plaza also honors the former minister and radio preacher who was a well-known Brooklyn activist.

A deteriorating brownstone church, designed by James Renwick in 1853, was razed in 1923 and replaced with the present Neo-Gothic stone sanctuary by Frank H. Quinby. Tiffany's nonfigurative window filled with shades of golden glass is placed above the pointed arch entrance to reflect the quiet spirit found within its doors.

Original wooden pews that seat four hundred line the cream-colored interior adorned with large opaque-glass windows and vaulted rib ceiling. Be sure to see the oak baptismal font dating to the founding flock. An unadorned dark wood altar table with matching reredos holds the Bible and brass candleholders. Look for two Tiffany windows that were salvaged from the Renwick church; especially beautiful is *The Adoration of the Magi*, which glows in shades of turquoise, lavender and white, with the infant Jesus bathed in golden light.

350 Clinton Avenue (between Lafayette and Vanderbilt Avenues), Brooklyn, NY 11238

EMMANUEL BAPTIST CHURCH

Charles Pratt, oil company owner and generous patron to many charitable causes, founded this congregation with more than 150 members from the Washington Avenue Baptist Church. The group was enraged by Pastor Emory J. Haynes, who published a satire on monopolies and the enormous wealth accumulated by businessmen. Pratt continued to criticize the minister until Haynes resigned and left Brooklyn. Since no expense was spared for the industrialists' new haven, the sanctuary is remembered as the "Standard Oil Church."

In the 1940s, black residents who were migrating from downtown Brooklyn began to integrate with the white congregation. The first black minister, Dr. H. Edward Whittaker, added gospel music in 1975, and today, there are three Sunday services for a huge congregation, which continues to play a vital role in community events, not unlike the church's founding fathers.

Architecture

This French Neo-Gothic landmark by Francis Hatch Kimball was built in 1886, with twin towers framing the triple-arched entrance, and was filled with decorative arches, multisized columns and lancet windows. Above the façade's huge Gothic window, a sculpture of St. John the Baptist is

Emmanuel Baptist Church entrance doors.

featured under the peaked roof, while a decorative lintel over the center door holds the congregation's name, Emmanuel (from Hebrew, meaning "God is with us"). Church archives report that the ornamental carvings of corbels, capitals, gargoyles and panels were created by South Brooklyn sculptor R.T. Heath. Look around the corner for a chapel with a round tower, erected in 1882. It was the site's first building designed by architect Ebenezer Roberts from Standard Oil, who also had built the former church, now Brown Memorial Baptist Church.

Upon entering the narthex, see the bronze angel guarding the bas-relief image of Charles Pratt and glance upward to the barrel-shaped mahogany ceiling restored to its original splendor. The nave's multicolored stained-glass windows and charming roundels line the sanctuary, while multitudes of angels can be found throughout the square-shaped interior with arch-styled seating. Six original brass chandeliers were once gas lights, and a dark wood gallery circling the nave is supported only by two brownstone columns in a sanctuary that is otherwise column-free. Upper green and gold stenciled walls were restored in 1998, while earth-toned lower walls were newly designed by architect Victor Body-Lawson with artistic Coptic crosses.

Since baptism is always by total immersion, the chancel is focused on a copper pool encircled by pink marble and placed behind the pulpit. Look above for an exquisite five-paneled window where you can almost hear the choir of angels that surrounds the image of Jesus as the Good Shepherd, chanting the window's inscription, "Praise Ye to the Lord, Praise Him All His Angels."

279 Lafayette Avenue (between Hall Street and St. James Place), Brooklyn, NY 11238; 718-622-1107

APOSTOLIC FAITH MISSION

Located next door to Emmanuel Baptist Church, this Christian sanctuary was built as the Orthodox Friends Meetinghouse in 1868 when there was dissension within the sect and is attributed to Stephen C. Earle. The building was sold in 1901 to Emmanuel, but the Friends utilized the sanctuary until 1955. Alterations to the original red brick Romanesque façade in 1902 added the stone cornice, Gothic quatrefoil panels and some newly shaped windows. The white stucco façade with wine-colored trim is surrounded by a black railing and has a green garden tucked into its corner space. Today's congregation purchased the site in 1965 and welcome all to this serene haven in the same spirit as the original Friends.

265 Lafayette Avenue (and Washington Avenue), Brooklyn, NY 11238; 718-622-2295

BROWN MEMORIAL BAPTIST CHURCH

Architect Ebenezer L. Roberts from the Standard Oil Company built this sanctuary in 1860 as Washington Avenue Baptist Church. The red brick Romanesque design with round archways and brownstone trim is anchored by a square turreted bell tower on its corner site. Here Charles Pratt and many of his associates worshiped for more than twenty years before moving to Emmanuel Baptist Church. Seventh-Day Adventists purchased the property in 1929 and remained until 1958. The present congregation that bought the building in 1959 traces its roots to Berean Missionary Baptist Church from 1851 in Crown Heights.

A mosaic triptych placed above the baptismal pool in the apse is the interior's focus. With outstretched arms, a full-length image of Jesus affirms "Come Unto Me," while Apostles Peter (holding his keys of leadership) and Paul (holding his sword to defend Christianity) are on either side. Triumphant angels hovering in a mural overhead adorn the triptych's archway. The high-vaulted nave, which includes a wood-faced gallery, can seat more than 1,500 worshipers and has varied styles of stained glass memorializing nineteenth-century ancestors, while small plaques on windowsills honor current members who care for this historic haven.

484 Washington Avenue (and Gates Avenue), Brooklyn, NY 11238; 718-638-6121

BY THE WAY

When walking along Washington Avenue, note other spiritual havens: Evergreen Church of God at 489, Zion Baptist Church built in 1949 at 527 and Bedford Zion Church founded in 1927 at 550 Washington Avenue.

CHURCH OF ST. LUKE AND ST. MATTHEW

The Episcopal congregation of St. Luke, which first organized on this site in 1841, built this enormous church in 1888 inspired by Italy's sanctuaries. The Italian Renaissance design by John Welch has myriad embellishments on its stone façade: a huge rose window with terra-cotta tracery, gables and spires, a round arch over the main entrance flanked by twin towers and lines of marble columns. An asymmetrical bell tower is filled with dozens of arches along with a cross on its pyramid-shaped roof that rises high above Clinton Avenue. This impressive landmark also has an intimate chapel with two thoughtful inscriptions over its portal: "To the Memory of an Only Child" and, on the entrance arch, "In His Name."

The decorative interior's apse, with its altar, reredos and windows, is from 1853, but nearly all of the nave's windows are by Tiffany and were installed beginning in 1896. Stories seen include Mary and Martha of Bethany tending to their visitor, Jesus, and powerful images of Archangels Gabriel and Michael are memorials to Henry Patchin Martin, a generous benefactor who died in 1906. The rose window, installed in 1890 and probably designed by the Italian-influenced architect, has a romantic roundel of chubby putti, sweet faces of young angels. It was a gift from the Sunday school children and a fitting tribute for the sanctuary that remains the largest of its sect on Long Island. St. Matthew's Church joined with the congregation in 1943 and placed its window of Apostle Matthew, as a former tax collector, in the chapel.

520 Clinton Avenue (between Atlantic and Fulton Street), Brooklyn, NY 11238; 718-638-0686

Prospect Heights

After 1870, when Prospect Park had been completed, upper-class residents moved into newly built limestone and brick homes and would welcome the 1910 opening of Brooklyn Botanic Garden on fifty-two acres. The area continued to grow with immigrant settlers who needed additional housing, as well as new sacred havens. By the late 1940s, the neighborhood had started to decline and was overrun with abandoned buildings, high crime rates and racial unrest. The city began the area's restoration effort by selling land for housing construction in the 1980s; it revived the neighborhood and attracted Caribbean immigrants who celebrated their roots with an annual Mardi Gras parade along Eastern Parkway. Residents continue to share the community with the Brooklyn Museum, dedicated in 1897, and Brooklyn Public Library, which opened in 1941. Eastern Parkway, along with Flatbush and Atlantic Avenues, acts as a fluid neighborhood boundary, with more than thirty-nine sacred sites within the area.

SOLDIERS' AND SAILORS' MEMORIAL ARCH

The Memorial Arch, designed by John H. Duncan in homage to the Arc de Triomphe in Paris, is a Civil War monument (1861–1865) that was unveiled by President Grover Cleveland in 1892. Surrounded by a wide roadway, the arch sits regally in Grand Army Plaza, which was designed by Olmsted and Vaux in 1862 as the entrance to Prospect Park. The portal is engraved "To

Frederick MacMonnies' bronzes on the Civil War Memorial Arch.

the Defenders of the Union" and features two pedestals with realistic clusters of army and navy forces that were designed by Frederick MacMonnies. Don't miss the bas-reliefs on the arch's inner walls: President Abraham Lincoln by Thomas Eakins and Union leader General Ulysses S. Grant by William O'Donovan. Visitors can arrange to walk up seventy-two feet to the top of the landmark arch for a closer look at the MacMonnies chariot and horse bronzes. Nearby Bailey Fountain is similar to water sculptures found in European cities, while the bust of America's thirty-fifth president, John F. Kennedy (1917–1963), holds his memorable inaugural quote: "Ask not what your country can do for you; ask what you can do for your country."

Flatbush Avenue and Eastern Parkway; 718-788-0055

UNION TEMPLE (KOL ISRAEL)

In 1848, Temple Beth Elohim, the first Jewish congregation on Long Island, was begun by German immigrants on Williamsburg's Keap Street, where its old synagogue is still utilized by the Pupa Hasidim. Temple Israel, which

Union Temple entrance doors.

formed in 1869, united with the group to begin this new Reform house of worship, hence the name.

Located near Grand Army Plaza, the eleven-story community center, designed by Arnold Brunner in 1925, was to have an adjoining synagogue, but the plan was cancelled by the financial depression of 1929. Its large auditorium, originally used for concerts, was converted into the sanctuary.

Look above the three exterior entrances for relevant sculptures of the menorah, the Decalogue and the Lions of Judah guarding the unrolled Torah. Upon entering the narthex, see the words chiseled in stone over brass doors as reminders of Judaic doctrine: "One God Above All" and "One Law One Humanity." Stained-glass windows were added in the 1940s and hold traditional icons, with one exception: the image of Moses with the Decalogue.

While adhering to the tenets of Judaism, the synagogue introduced innovations attributed to the freedom flowing in America and continued to adjust to the spirit of Reform Judaism through the years. Interfaith families, the gay community and youth groups are warmly welcomed, while the equality of women is exemplified by religious leader Dr. Linda Henry Goodman.

17 Eastern Parkway, Brooklyn, NY 11238; 718-638-7600

Prospect Park

The people of Brooklyn love their landmark recreational park, while millions of visitors enjoy its diversity and the many peaceful spots to rest their spirits. More than five hundred acres were set aside for this public park, skillfully designed by Olmsted and Vaux in 1867. Its administrative center, Litchfield Villa (Prospect Park West at 5th Street; 718-965-8951), which was inherited with the land tract, was built by architect A.J. Davis in the 1850s as a country home for railroad magnate Edwin Litchfield, who was the major landowner of today's park. Lefferts Homestead, a Dutch home rebuilt in 1783 and donated to the city by the Lefferts family, was moved into the park in 1918 from Flatbush Avenue. Peter Lefferts served in the Continental army and was a delegate to the Constitutional Convention. The original home from 1776 was burned in the Battle of Long Island to prevent British occupation.

Prospect Lake, a man-made body of water, offers boat rides, while a popular tennis center welcomes individuals and sports leagues. The renovated Wolman Ice Rink has evolved into Lakeside, a year-round recreational facility, and the zoo's brick buildings still have interior murals from the 1940s. Prospect Park Audubon Center was opened in 2002 when the National Audubon Society started an official center for birdwatchers. The park can be entered in many locations, but go to the Boathouse Information Center, where maps and special events listings are available, and enjoy free guided tours every Saturday led by park rangers.

Friends Burial Ground

Located within Prospect Park, this ten-acre cemetery is on private property that the Friends congregation owned when Brooklyn was a city and when the land tract was not a park. A posted sign estimates that it was opened between 1849 and 1851. The Friends' first meetinghouse was built in Brooklyn Heights in 1835, while the second house from 1857 is still active in downtown Brooklyn (see entry). This burial ground is the resting place of church elders, and also buried there is popular film actor Montgomery Clift, whose site is a well-kept secret. Low-rise, rectangular gray headstones sit gently among trees surrounded by a black iron fence. Although the cemetery isn't open to the public, you can still look into the private grounds near the park's 16th Street entrance.

JAPANESE HILL-AND-POND GARDEN

A blood-orange Torii gate rises out of the water to mark the entry to the sacred haven of the Shinto gods of nature (the kami). They are represented by water, trees or flowers but never in human form. The gate, with the Japanese inscription "Dai-myo-jin" ("Spirit of Light"), alerts visitors that the shrine is in the nearby pine grove filled with evergreens to symbolize eternity and flowering plants for the fleeting nature of life. Wooden bridges, stone lanterns and a viewing pavilion add special touches to grounds, which cover more than three acres.

The garden was first built in 1915 by Japanese immigrant Takeo Shiota (1881–1943). He paid homage to the Miyajima gate standing in the Inland Sea of Japan but added bronze cranes as a quirky American touch. Takeo was from Ohtaki Chiba and wrote to his family that his soul would always live in this garden.

Takeo Shiota died on December 3, 1943, in a Japanese internment camp in South Carolina, and his original shrine was burned in 1937 because of anti-Japanese sentiment. It was reopened in 1947 and was restored throughout the years, but in June 2000, the garden underwent another major renovation. Be sure to begin your tour at the ten-foot stone lantern more than 350 years old, a gift from Tokyo in 1980, and don't miss Turtle Island, named for the sunbathers along the rocky water edge. The botanical complex has more than fifty-two acres and twelve thousand plants, but the Japanese garden remains a sacred space filled with the spirits of the kami and of Takeo Shiota.

1000 Washington Avenue (at Eastern Parkway), Brooklyn, NY 11225; 718-623-7200

ST. JOSEPH ROMAN CATHOLIC CHURCH

In 1850, Bishop John Hughes (1797–1864), who presided over the Archdiocese of New York and Long Island, started this parish for local families, who had raised $500, and dedicated a small church three years later. Architect Francis J. Berlenbach designed today's Italian Renaissance brick sanctuary in 1921, with two handsome copper-capped towers and all the symmetry that identifies its style. Granite steps lead to an impressive portico with polished stone columns and terra-cotta arches, all in tribute to the determination of the founding congregation.

An elaborate barrel-vaulted interior that is eighty-eight feet wide and more than two hundred feet long is filled with antique oak pews and a towering Italian marble baldachin more than forty feet high. It is engraved "Ite Ad Joseph" ("Go to Joseph") and crowned with a statue of the patron,while winged angels sound their trumpets from each corner. Glorious colored marbles, green-veined columns and sienna-toned wainscoting add to the interior beauty created by Domenico Borgia. See the stained-glass window *Workshop of Nazareth*, with Joseph from the House of David laboring at his carpentry trade while a young Jesus talks with his mother, Mary. All mural paintings and figurative windows were designed by Alexander F. Locke.

856 Pacific Street (between Vanderbilt and Underhill Avenues), Brooklyn, NY 11238; 718-783-4500

St. Teresa of Avila

Reverend Joseph McNamee was sent to this Irish immigrant neighborhood in 1874 to start a church in the middle of green fields. The small congregation purchased the present site from the Lefferts estate and constructed the lower church itself. It would take thirteen years for the upper sanctuary, able to seat more than 1,500, to be completed.

The Italianate stucco façade, having symmetrical copper towers added in 1905, was remodeled in 1947, with the major addition of a portico faced with three stained-glass windows. Church records from the 1940s indicate that there were more than three thousand men and women from the parish who served in armed forces. Fittingly, the portico windows by John Keller & Son became memorials to servicemen, with the inscription, "To those who served, our constant gratitude. To those who sacrificed, our reverent esteem. For all who gave their lives, a prayerful remembrance…"

In 1949, an interior renovation added the green marble baldachin with gold-leaf pillars over the altar table. Look up to see the circular stained-glass window highlighting the founding congregation's Celtic cross, as well as the portrait of Christ as king dominating the sky-blue rounded apse. Patron Teresa (1515–1582), from the small city of Avila, was a Spanish Carmelite nun and mystic whose writings are celebrated as masterpieces (including *Interior Castle* and *Way of Perfection*). The former Teresa Sanchez de Cepeda y Alhumada had a Jewish grandfather among her large Castilian family and never lost her compassion for people. Look for her marble image and mural painting in the chancel, as well as a glistening white statue outside the rectory. Services are held in English, French Creole and Spanish, reflecting the census of today's parish.

563 Sterling Place (between Classon and Franklin Avenues), Brooklyn, NY 11238; 718-622-6500

ST. PETER CLAVER

Imbedded in the church's history is the story of American segregation. The Colored Roman Catholic Club of Brooklyn began in 1915 and functioned until World War I intervened. At the end of the war, Reverend Bernard J. Quinn (1883–1940), who had returned from overseas as an army chaplain, and Jules DeWeever (1871–1940), Dutch West Indies immigrant and lay leader, searched for former members, gathered them together and made plans for a formal church in 1920. Segregation was still the norm within society and churches, but Quinn devoted his life to ministering to the black population. He said, "It seems to me that no church can exclude anyone and still keep its Christian ideals."

The diocese purchased the current site, originally built as a Congregational church but well known as a bus and truck depot. After extensive restorations, the Brooklyn diocese dedicated the red brick sanctuary as Church of St. Theresa of the Little Flower for Colored Brethren in 1922. The congregation supported a Long Island orphanage along with summer camp for children that would evolve into one of New York City's largest social service agencies. But it would not be without problems, as bigots would successfully burn down the camp two times. Father Quinn never feared and utilized fireproof material for the third building. It remains in use today.

In 1925, the group name was changed to honor Peter Claver (1581–1654), a Jesuit priest who spent his entire ministry attending to cargos of African slaves that landed every month at Cartagena in the Caribbean. He instructed them through interpreters, brought them food and is said to have baptized more than 300,000 captives before they were sold and shipped to foreign ports. Look over the church entrance and on the auditorium's corner site for sculptures of Claver pouring baptismal water on a slave's forehead.

Claver's story also fills the apse's mural, which surrounds a three-dimensional sculpture of the Crucifixion. Included in the historic mural is the story of twenty-two Roman Catholic martyrs of Uganda. There were

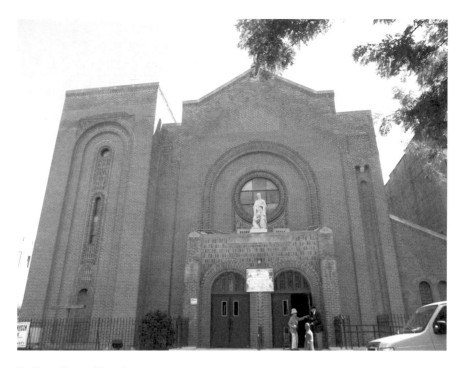

St. Peter Claver Church.

also twenty-three white Anglicans killed, and all the victims' deaths, between 1885 to 1887, are remembered today in Uganda with a national holiday.

Until his death, Father Quinn continued to exemplify the virtues of Peter Claver, leading his congregation with teachings of social justice and shielding them from racial confrontations. His portrait is prominently displayed in the nave, and his story is still being told by the neighborhood's oral historians.

29 Claver Place (Ormand Place and Jefferson Avenue), Brooklyn, NY 11238; 718-574-5772

Park Slope

Located on the western edge of Prospect Park, this residential area once sloped down from the park toward the harbor, hence its name. Park Slope started to develop in the 1870s after Prospect Park was completed and greatly expanded after the Brooklyn Bridge opened in 1883. It became an enclave of wealthy businessmen, who built homes and private clubs like the Venetian-style Montauk Club on 8th Avenue. Row houses and apartments were added for the mainly Irish immigrant laborers, but the area went into decline after World War II; it was revived again in the 1970s by young families seeking affordable housing, and as a result, architectural gems from the more prosperous years were preserved. More than thirty sacred havens were ushered into this historic district by congregations escaping downtown commercialism and by Park Slope descendants who would rebuild older sanctuaries for newer settlers.

ST. AUGUSTINE'S ROMAN CATHOLIC CHURCH

The *Brooklyn Eagle* reported that the Parfitt brothers (Albert, Walter and Henry), architects of this English Gothic and High Victorian sanctuary, were proud participants at the cornerstone dedication on November 12, 1888. The congregation, founded in 1870, had sold its property on Bergen Street and 5th Avenue to the Union Elevated Railway Company and opened this new sanctuary in 1892, farther up the slope.

St Augustine's glass-filled choir loft.

While Gabriel sounds his trumpet from a red tile rooftop, copper gargoyles and carved cherubs guard the handsome brownstone exterior. Enter through the portal in the bell tower and stop by the chapel to see the original baptistery, with stained-glass windows by Alexander Locke (1860–1921). Its marble walls hold tributes to twentieth-century leaders who sought justice and equality: Archbishop Oscar Romero of San Salvador, slain in 1980 while presiding at church services, and four women—Ita Ford and Maura Clarke, both Maryknoll missionaries; Dorothy Kazel of the Ursuline Order; and lay worker Jean Donovan—all brutally murdered in 1980 by members of El Salvador's National Guard. See prophets of nonviolence Mahatma (meaning "teacher" or "great soul") Gandhi, the Hindu leader who led India to resist its British overlords; New Yorker Dorothy Day, who cofounded the Catholic worker movement in 1933 with Peter Maurin; and Southern Baptist civil rights leader Dr. Martin Luther King Jr., killed in 1968.

Before you enter the cruciform nave, look at the tympana over entry doors for Tiffany's art glass featuring flowering vines and tetramorphs of the four evangelists: Mark as a winged lion; Matthew, the winged man; John, the eagle; and Luke, the winged ox. Dozens of cherubs are poised along the molding, and it is said that more than six hundred angels are hovering throughout the church. The elaborate sanctuary with vaulted ribbed ceiling and wide arches holding clerestory windows is flooded with glorious light from more than one hundred figurative stained-glass windows, door inserts and skylights. Seven opalescent windows above the reredos by local artisan Locke tell of the life of Jesus.

At the nave's entrance, the baptismal font is encircled by a wooden arch holding painted images of twelve remarkable Christians, among them Elizabeth Seton, Thomas More, Kateri Tekawitha and Lorenzo Ruiz of the Phillipines. The choir loft above the baptistery showcases Locke's six lancet windows of church notables associated with music: King David of Israel, with his harp; Pope Gregory, creator of Gregorian chant; and Catherine of Bologna (1413–1463), composer of hymns, shown with her violin.

The most interesting set of Locke's six windows on the north and south sides of the nave tells of Augustine of Hippo (354–430), author of *City of God* and *Confessions of St. Augustine*, and his mother, Monica, who prayed that her son would leave his life of debauchery. One window features Augustine struggling with the doctrine of the Trinity when he meets a child on a beach trying to empty the ocean's water into a hole. The window is inscribed: "Child, you cannot turn the sea into that hole," says Augustine. "Neither can you comprehend the Trinity," the child answers.

Today, the church continues to welcome its Spanish, French, Asian and English-speaking congregation, which is fondly represented with a motto from St. Augustine: "Amid the various languages of men, the faith of the heart speaks one tongue."

116 6th Avenue (between Sterling and Park Places), Brooklyn, NY 11217; 718-783-3132

OLD FIRST REFORMED CHURCH

This is the fifth home of the original Dutch Collegiate Reformed Church, which ruled Brooklyn for more than 125 years. The name "Reformed" recognizes the sixteenth-century European Reformation, which separated the protestors, or Protestant sects, from the Roman Catholic Church. Stern Dutch leader Peter Stuyvesant (1610–1672) had to grant permission to form a church, which forced other sects to secretly worship. As the sixth and last director-general from 1647 to 1664, Stuyvesant surrendered to

British forces in 1664, and the English were more tolerant of some sects but not all.

In 1886, the entire block between Carroll and President Streets was purchased by this congregation and a chapel built on the site. It evolved into this huge Neo-Gothic sanctuary designed by George L. Morse in 1893 and topped by a two-hundred-foot tower that's the focal point of the neighborhood.

The arched nave that's shaped like a Greek Cross, with arms of equal length, rises more than sixty feet to a stenciled plaster ceiling with wooden ribs. See the Virgilio Tojetti (1851–1901) painting *The Empty Tomb*, a reminder that women always stay when life gets difficult; it is placed on the reredos above gilded panels inscribed with the Ten Commandments. Most glorious is the diverse collection of stained glass that filters colorful light into the huge sanctuary with seating for 1,200. Otto Heiniske, Tiffany Studios, William Willet and anonymous artists created art glass filled with Christian stories and as memorials for old Brooklyn families. See the balcony's rose window, created by an unknown artist, with the Guardian Angel roundel; the memorial by William Willet for physician Theodore Mason, one of the organizers of Long Island College Hospital; and the Tiffany work remembering Jacques Cortelyou, surveyor general of the early Dutch government. The arts-and-craft interior is further illuminated by the once gas-operated "Great Chandelier," which is now a work of art in itself. The church remains a living history book rooted in seventeenth-century Dutch colonial government and continues as an eyewitness to New York's twenty-first-century diversity.

127 7th Avenue (Between Carroll and President Streets), Brooklyn, NY 11215; 718-638-8300

St. Francis Xavier Roman Catholic Church

In 1886, Reverend David J. Hickey, founding pastor who served the congregation until his death in 1937, named the new parish for his alma mater, St. Francis Xavier College in Manhattan. He first leased a brownstone for services, then built a small sanctuary covered in galvanized metal, which caused him to be known as the "tin church" pastor.

The present Gothic Revival granite building, trimmed with limestone, was started in 1900 and designed by Thomas F. Houghton with a massive tower placed at its west end and winged gargoyles guarding the rooftop. In the arched tympanum over the main entry, Patron Francis (1506–1552) is seen preaching in Asia during his ministry. He was born a nobleman in Navarre, Spain, and studied philosophy in Paris at the College of St. Barbara, where he met Ignatius of Loyola. He joined with him to found the Order of Jesus, known as the Jesuits, and spent most of his life traveling, converting many to Christianity and dying in 1541 in Goa, India, where he is buried.

The colorful interior extends 167 feet in length and 110 feet in width, with a traditional rose window featuring the harpist King David of Israel surrounded by angels playing the lute, lyre and, rarely seen, drums. Multicolored marble columns supporting arcades rise to the vaulted ceiling accented with colorful ribbing. Flags from parishioners' nations, stained-glass stories and recessed sculptures of the fourteen Stations of the Cross add exquisite texture to the interior. The glistening white reredos has three spiral canopies that hold marble statues carved by prolific sculptor Vincent Fucignas. Two large windows honor Francis: one tells of his death in Goa, and the other his arrival on the shores of Japan.

Be sure to see the triptych (three panels) of Mary with the child Jesus in the chapel just off Carroll Street. In the 1860s, it was given to the family of George W. Hennings by Giuseppe Garibaldi, a leader for Italy's unification movement, in thanks for aiding his campaign. Edwina Hennings Brose donated the artifact to the parish when the new church was being erected. She was not a parishioner nor from a Catholic family, but she found an appropriate home for the historical gift.

225 6ᵗʰ Avenue (between Carroll and President Streets), Brooklyn, NY 11215; 718-638-1880

THREE CHURCHES

Gothic Revival churches reside on each corner where 6ᵗʰ and 7ᵗʰ Avenues intersect with St. John's Place (once Douglass Street but renamed in 1870). The churches were witnesses to the 1960 United Airlines plane crash and supported the workers at the scene. Every Sunday at 11:00 a.m., this corner echoes with prayer and music emanating from all three sanctuaries.

St. John's Episcopal Church, organized in 1827, resembles an English country haven, with trefoil windows set into dormers. Placed within a garden, the Victorian Gothic church's main entrance has seven lancet windows within the brownstone and rough ashlar façade. It was designed in 1885 by John R. Thomas, who built over 150 churches but is well known for the Surrogate's Courthouse (Hall of Records) in Manhattan. The chapel addition in 1870 is by Edward Tuckerman Potter. The parish was begun by Reverend Evan Malbone Johnson on this corner of his farm, where he built a wooden church to serve an integrated congregation. He was a staunch abolitionist who served his congregation for twenty years. Surely Johnson would rejoice to see how his church grew while remaining a multiracial parish that welcomes all to services.

139 St. John's Place (between 6th and 7th Avenues), Brooklyn, NY 11217; 718-783-3928

Iglesia Presbiteriana (Memorial Presbyterian Church) was founded by thirty-three members of Lafayette Presbyterian Church (see entry) in 1866 as a mission chapel. The 1882 Victorian Gothic brownstone design by Pugin & Walter measures ninety-five by sixty-seven feet and is anchored by a buttressed tower with a tall steeple rising above its blue slate roof. Walk through the tower's entrance into the narthex, which is separated from the nave by a high dark wood gate with open arches. Glorious Tiffany windows

Memorial Presbyterian Church.

in the cream-colored interior are everywhere, filling both the church and chapel with peaceful beauty. Look for Tiffany angels in single lancets and at the Resurrection Tomb. Study the disbelieving Peter being rescued by Jesus from his walk on rough waters of Galilee. On the chapel wall, see the red-garbed Jesus with turquoise shawl surrounded by happy children. Tiffany art glass enhances door panels and a wall of windows added in 1888 that divides the nave from the chapel. Circular pews able to seat eight hundred face an apse with its wood screen filled with Gothic arches and trefoil circles. Hispanic services are now held in the sanctuary, and the church shares its space for a day-care center and neighborhood meetings.

186 St. John's Place (and 7th Avenue), Brooklyn, NY 11217; 718-638-5541

Grace United Methodist Church has a large pinnacled tower that lost its spire during a 1944 hurricane. The Gothic Victorian brownstone by the Parfitt brothers was built in 1882, with exterior windows framed in terra cotta. Look along St. John's Place for a textured façade, arched windows and decorative stone buttresses. Note the hexagram, an omen of good fortune, on the tympanum. The cream-colored interior is lined with thin marble columns that support the clerestory's circular windows, while scenic stained-glass windows surround the lower nave. A carved dark wood altar and reredos are set into an unadorned apse surrounded by a Gothic arch, and it is here that the only figurative window is found: Jesus reaching out his arms to the congregation.

The group traces its beginnings to 1866, when its 7th Avenue sanctuary was sold due to overwhelming debt. In 1878, it changed the name to Grace Methodist Episcopal Church and financed this structure. In 1960, there would be another name change, to United Methodist. It was the freedom flowing in America that established the Methodist sect in Manhattan during 1768.

33 7th Avenue and St. John's Place, Brooklyn, NY 11217; 718-230-0777

THE STONE HOUSE MUSEUM

One of the bloodiest encounters from the American Revolution's Battle of Brooklyn took place on this site. In 1776, George Washington's troops, surrounded by British forces and German mercenaries, were forced to escape across the foggy East River, with their flank protected by four hundred colonial soldiers from Maryland. It is estimated that 256 soldiers died in the battle commanded by Mordechai Grist and were buried in unmarked graves.

The historical stone house, property of the Nicholas Vechte family, was originally located beside Gowanus Creek and belonged to the seventeenth-century Dutch town of New Utrecht. Its reconstruction on this nearby site was led by Borough President J.J. Byrne in 1933, for whom the park was renamed, but in December 2008, it reverted to its original designation honoring George Washington. The house, now holding programs commemorating Brooklyn's history, was also utilized by the Brooklyn Baseball Club, which played in the park during 1854 before evolving into the Brooklyn Dodgers in 1883.

3rd Street (between 4th and 5th Avenues), PO Box 150613, Brooklyn, NY 11215; 718-768-3195

CONGREGATION BETH ELOHIM (HOUSE OF GOD)

Founded in downtown Brooklyn in 1861 by German immigrants, this Reform congregation relocated to this site in 1909 to escape noisy commercialism. The group built the first synagogue in Park Slope, this classical Roman-style limestone temple designed by Eisendrath and Horowitz. It's often referred to as the Garfield Temple, indicating its location.

The impressive main entrance, sitting cater-corner on the large site, is flanked by Ionic columns and black wrought-iron menorahs. Look up to see the Shield of David piercing the skyline atop the dome. An enormous stained-glass window dominates the recessed entry, while above the entrance, an engraved phrase reads, "Mine house shall be a house of prayer for all people."

The oval-shaped interior is filled with light from figurative stained-glass windows that recognized the freedom flowing in America. Look for white-robed Moses receiving the Ten Commandments and the huge, colorful window of baby Moses being rescued from the bulrushes by the Egyptian pharaoh's daughter and her handmaidens. She would call the child Moses because he came from the water. The sacred ark is surrounded by a marble portal reflecting the exterior design and is seemingly protected by two enormous golden columns.

Temple House, an Art Deco community center built in 1928 across the street from the synagogue, has an intimate Old World chapel for Friday night services. See antique English stained-glass windows by John Tarbox & Company that tell Old Testament stories: *Mercy*, showing travel-weary Elijah

Interior of Beth Elohim.

receiving food from a widow; *Justice*, with an ancient judge reading egalitarian law to a trio including a begger, a richly robed trader and an African man; and *Humility*, depicting Moses standing before the burning bush.

274 Garfield Place (8th Avenue and Prospect Park West), Brooklyn, NY 11215; 718-768-7414

PARK SLOPE CHRISTIAN TABERNACLE

Representative of storefronts transformed into chapels, this sacred haven was founded by immigrants from Puerto Rico who arrived in the 1950s. Members, originally on 4th Avenue, purchased the present site, which was renovated into a modern sanctuary. It accommodates about ninety worshipers, with services conducted in Spanish and English. Several storefront chapels in the vicinity also serve small congregations.

5th Avenue between Flatbush Avenue and Union Street

St. Thomas Aquinas Roman Catholic Church

Original stained glass over the tripartite entrance and in the nave's windows attest to the age of this Early Gothic red brick haven built in 1885. A chapel that houses the baptistery was opened the following year along 8th Street, but it would only be in 2005 that the chapel's stained glass was installed by artisans Jacek and Renata Olechowski of Galahad Studios.

Carved wood pews and original wainscoting fill the warm interior, which is focused on an enormous wooden cross hanging above the chancel. Two stained-glass windows tell of Patron Thomas. As a writer, he is shown with the crucified Jesus, who is whispering, "You have written well of me." As a priest, he is kneeling at the altar and participating in the Eucharist. As a preacher, he is shown with the image of the Holy Spirit inspiring his lecture to other religious leaders. Patron Thomas (1226–1274), a brilliant student and son of the Count of Aquino, joined the Order of St. Dominic at the age of seventeen and continued his studies at Cologne under St. Albert the Great. Although he was called "Dumb Ox" because of his shy way and ample body, Thomas became a great preacher and prolific writer who left to posterity *Summa Theologica*, a masterpiece revered by theology and philosophy students.

Art glass works painted with antique geometric patterns in misty colors were early windows that were probably meant to be replaced; church records state that windows were made in Innsbuck, Austria, without identifying which ones were imported.

Look in the nave's small shrine, filled with saintly images that reflect past and present congregations: St. Patrick, holding his green shamrock for the Irish; St. Francis Cabrini, with her books that educated Italian immigrants; the richly clothed Madonna of Cisne, for the Ecuadorians; Madonna of Cuba, shown protecting fishermen at sea; and Madonna of Guadalupe from Mexico. As you leave, see the narthex's windows inscribed with "Porta Coeli" ("Gateway to Heaven"), still a fitting tribute to this church that remains the bridge to America for immigrants.

249 9th Street (and 4th Avenue), Brooklyn, NY 11215; 718-768-9471

HOLY NAME OF JESUS

Services were initially held at the nearby Thom McCann shoe factory until the present corner site was purchased for the Roman Catholic Irish congregation, founded in 1878 by Reverend Thomas D. Reilly, who led the church for forty years until his death.

The red brick Gothic interior still has its vaulted wooden ceiling, Gothic arches and Corinthian pillars lining the sanctuary, but the entire apse has been radically renovated with new lighting fixtures and a modern altar. Original stained glass fills the clerestory, while lower windows hold quotes from the Bible. "I and the Father Are One," reads a sacred inscription inserted within colorful glass panes. In the exterior garden, a sparkling white tableau of the Crucifixion is a reminder of the ultimate sacrifice of Jesus, with its life-size figures easily spotted on the avenue.

245 Prospect Park West (and Windsor Place), Brooklyn, NY 11215; 718-768-3071

THE VIRGIN MARY OF THE ARAB MELKITE RITE

Syrian Catholic immigrants of the Byzantine-Melkite (Greek) Rite gathered for worship on Washington Street in Lower Manhattan in the early 1900s before members migrated to Brooklyn. They first worshiped in 1910 on the lower level of St. Paul's Church on Court Street (see entry), relocating to Park Slope in 1922 and finally arriving on this site in 1950.

To meet the cultural and liturgical needs of the rapidly growing group, Reverend Elias B. Skaff purchased the present Victorian Gothic haven from the Park Slope Congregational Church, which was built in 1904. The building is anchored by a corner tower with three distinct entrances, enhancing the exterior design. The gray granite façade has been embellished with a mosaic of Patron Mary and her young son, Jesus.

To accommodate traditional symbolism, the interior was skillfully renovated while keeping the original cruciform footprint intact. Byzantine portraits surround *Christ Pantocrator* (*Great High Priest*) in a shallow gilded dome that supports the crystal chandelier. Huge figurative windows left by the former congregation fill the apse and side walls. The congregation installed the bronze and mosaic iconostatis, and imbedded in the wood façade of the curved balcony, fourteen small golden plaques tell the journey of Jesus to his death. As you leave, see the golden icon of John the Baptist and the figurative windows installed by members who created this Byzantine haven.

216 8ᵗʰ Avenue (and 2ⁿᵈ Street), Brooklyn, NY 11215; 718-788-5454

PARK SLOPE JEWISH CENTER

Congregation of Tifereth Israel, founded in 1900, built this center in 1925, identifying its ritual as egalitarian Conservative Judaism. Two nearby congregations would unite with them: B'nai Jacob, founded in 1873, joined in 1942; and B'nai Sholaum, founded in 1888, merged in 1960.

The light brick Romanesque building, whose façade is filled with a traditional wheel window high above a row of lancets, still retains its intimate interior, with details that have never been altered from the original design. A mural of the sunrise is placed over the sacred ark, and the nave's stained-glass oculus has kept its colorful Shield of David that was intended to raise your eyes toward the heavens. Banks of windows flood the sanctuary with light, while original brass light fixtures add charming touches. Restoration of this historic building is an ongoing priority for members.

8ᵗʰ Avenue and 14ᵗʰ Street Brooklyn, NY 11215; 718-768-1453

6ᵀᴴ AVENUE HAVENS

Walk along 6ᵗʰ Avenue and see its skyline dotted with steeples. There are more than 150 Baptists churches in Brooklyn because there is no hierarchy in Baptist churches, and congregations can be started where needed. Greenwood Baptist Church, founded in 1858, sits cater-corner on the busy avenue, with its huge stone crenellated tower that holds its entrance (461 6ᵗʰ Avenue). The Sixth Avenue Baptist Church is a red brick Gothic church built in 1880 by Lawrence Valk with spires but no steeple, due to a 1938 hurricane (6ᵗʰ Avenue and Lincoln Place; 718-638-1411).

Red Hook

R ed Hook, once a thriving waterfront industrial district, remains isolated from mainland Brooklyn by tunnels and expressways and has never lost its maritime ambience. With no direct subway line, visitors must ride the only bus, B61, from Jay Street in downtown Brooklyn to see buildings from the nineteenth to the twenty-first century. Red Hook Houses, a public housing project built in the 1930s with thirty buildings and more than eight thousand tenants, severely contrasts with two- and three-story residences and represents a huge percentage of the population. Artists are creating another layer in the community as they restore old homes, develop galleries and open cafés. In 2004, plans were announced by Swedish furniture giant IKEA to develop the twenty-two-acre shipyard site; it promised better transit connections, free weekend ferry service and jobs. After finishing the complex, the first investment in Red Hook since World War II, the company was true to its word. For a peaceful interlude, you can ride the IKEA weekend ferry to and from South Street Seaport in Manhattan.

What's in the area's name? Native Americans called the area *Ihepetonga* ("high sandy bank"). Dutch settlers called it *Roode Hoek* ("red point," for the color of its soil). Following Dutch tradition, landholders cut the first canal to Gowanus Creek to make travel easier to the rest of Long Island. Gowanus Creek ran into New York Bay, and its name has two origins: Gowane, a leader of the Canarsees tribe who lived throughout Brooklyn and sold land to the Dutch in 1636, or *gouwee*, Dutch for "bay." During the American Revolutionary War, Fort Defiance on Beard Street fired on British frigate

HMS *Roebuck* from its high hill and kept the East River passageway open during the Battle of Long Island. Its site is thought to be located within Louis Valentino Jr. Park.

Irish and German immigrants began to arrive in the 1840s, along with Scandinavian sailors. In the 1880s, Italians started working on the piers and setting up food markets. In the 1920s, Puerto Ricans joined the busy area, which included what we know as Cobble Hill and Carroll Gardens. The waterfront employed a huge number of workers from 1840 to the 1950s to unload cargo, repair ships and work in the gasworks, coal yards, factories and tanneries.

Red Hook's distinctive hook was created by developers as a breakwater for ships in the port once called Erie Basin, while Gowanus Creek would be widened for industrial use after the Civil War. In 1942, many homes and churches were razed for the Gowanus Expressway, and the area divided into two neighborhoods, Red Hook and Gowanus. In 1950, the entrance of Brooklyn Battery Tunnel was opened at Hamilton Avenue, demolishing even more homes. Major shippers left the city in the 1960s. *Last Exit to Brooklyn*, written by native Hubert Selby Jr., echoed the story of a dying port when poverty, street gangs and organized crime ruled the waterfront. Today, a small number of sacred havens has tenaciously survived the industrial and demographic shift in the neighborhood and welcomes the renewal of Red Hook Terminal for the community.

VISITATION OF THE BLESSED VIRGIN MARY

This Roman Catholic congregation was founded in 1854 by Reverend Timothy O'Farrell for Irish immigrants who had been holding services in the Gilbride residence at Van Brunt and Sullivan Streets. They built a small brick church one year later. In 1878, a new church was dedicated, but sadly, the first service was to bury its founder; later, a devastating fire would consume nearly everything but the massive stone walls. In 1898, a group of businessmen engaged Patrick C. Keely to rebuild the church and add the prominent bell tower with four clocks. When Italian immigrants arrived in the parish, their colorful outdoor processions added another dimension to rituals.

The interior sanctuary, seating more than 1,200, features fourteen German stained-glass windows dedicated to events in the life of the patron Mary and her son, Jesus. Mary is also seen presenting to the thirteenth-

Visitation of the Blessed Virgin Sanctuary.

century Carmelite St. Simon Stock, a scapular (two small pieces of cloth holding sacred images); they were attached on the ends of a long ribbon. This vision of Simon popularized the wearing of scapulars and promoted homage to Mary under the title of Our Lady of Mount Carmel.

Be sure to see fourteen Old Testament murals lining the ceiling, including Elijah with his flaming chariot, Moses holding the Ten Commandments while dividing the Red Sea, Jonah and the whale and Noah with his ark. Dominating the apse is a huge mural of Calvary Hill detailing the death of Jesus. Tiffany is represented with four windows in the vestry, available only to the clergy, but there is one in the entry hall portraying Jesus as the Good Shepherd in a sparkling white robe. The Tiffany baptismal font with inlaid mosaics is in the chancel near the main altar.

Before you leave, look up to the tongue-and-groove strips on the dark wooden ceiling. Only shipbuilders could have shaped this hull as a lasting tribute to the seafarers and tradesmen from the Red Hook docks.

98 Richards Street (Van Brunt Street), Brooklyn, NY 11231; 718-624-1572

PART I

COFFEY PARK

Directly across from Visitation Church, this New York City park is an ideal spot to refresh your spirit. Opening in 1901, it was enlarged in 1907 and 1943 and given a major renovation in 1999. The park is named for Michael J. Coffey (1839–1907), who was an Irish immigrant who served as Democratic district leader for thirty-nine years and held public offices as alderman and state senator. Nearby Coffey Street also honors his memory.

PUBLIC PIERS AND PLACES

Be sure to visit the Louis J. Valentino Jr. Park and Pier at the end of Coffey Street, with its own walkway overlooking the East River. Some local historians think that this is the Revolutionary War site of Fort Defiance. The park is now a testimonial to a selfless firefighter who died in 1996 while searching in a burning building for his fellow firemen. You'll see glorious sights of Manhattan from the pier, as well as the full face of Lady Liberty. Beard Street Pier, at the end of Van Brunt Street, also offers peaceful meditation spots.

While walking on Van Brunt, look for the Veterans of Foreign Wars (VFW) Memorial from World War I. The oversized bronze statue of the enlisted soldier, called a doughboy, stands next to the VFW Hall between Sullivan and King Streets. Be sure to visit the Waterfront Museum and Showboat Barge at the foot of Conover Street, founded to preserve the waterfront and its seafaring history, as well as offer a stage to local performing artists.

KENTLER INTERNATIONAL DRAWING SPACE

A quiet haven for artists presents monthly exhibitions in a brick building that was originally a street-level habadashery in a private home. Having once served as a church, the gallery is now filled with work from local and international artists selected by its resident director and artist, Florence Neal. The space was opened in 1990, made possible by many supporters, including the New York State Council of the Arts through the Brooklyn Arts Council.

The façade of the four-story red brick building holds the name of the original Red Hook owners, the Kentler family, along with the date 1854.

William Kentler arrived from Germany at age seventeen, married Rosanna Smith from Ireland and opened his dry goods store to sell supplies to seafaring men. The Kentler descendants still live in Brooklyn and remember swimming off nearby docks. It is open Saturday from 1:00 p.m. to 4:00 p.m.; all other days are by appointment only.

353 Van Brunt Street (between Wolcott and Dikeman Streets), Brooklyn, NY 11231; 718-875-2098

The Kentler Gallery, built in 1854.

RED HOOK PENTECOSTAL HOLINESS CHURCH

Time stands still for this large Gothic building from 1899. It sits alone, echoing memories of a deserted port, with an old bell that probably called sailors to services hanging next to an exterior chimney. Records indicate that the bell once belonged to the fire department from the town of New Utrecht.

The Pentecostal Christian community is now in residence in the sanctuary founded by Christ Episcopal Church (see entry) on Clinton Street. Dr. Eli H. Canfield opened this mission in 1867 to work among immigrants and transient sailors near the docks. The site was purchased from the Atlantic Dock Company, and a chapel was built by Richard Upjohn & Son. Sunday school, sewing classes and a lending library, as well as clothing distribution, were part of the chapel's programs.

To keep up with the growing community, the congregation engaged architects William and George Audsley to design the present red brick English Gothic Revival church. The exterior's projecting vestibule, ornamented with a handsome terra-cotta arcade, has entrances on either side and three lancet windows filled with softly colored glass. Wood-framed pebble-glass doors lead into an open rectangular sanctuary with nary a column or arch in sight. The ceiling has exposed timber trusses, and light filters in through more than a dozen pairs of lancet windows tinted in pastel tones. Two wheel windows

Red Hook Pentecostal.

add decorative color—one dominates the sanctuary's façade, and the other, with a small roundel of Jesus, is featured in the apse.

Although there is no written evidence, it seems that the architects, noted for their creative ideas of ornamentation, would have been involved in designing the sanctuary's woodwork and art glass. The chancel retains all its original woodwork, and the narthex remains filled with artistic panels of colorful glass. George Audsley was famous for designing the Wanamaker pipe organ in Philadelphia.

Be sure to find the six-pointed star, an ancient Byzantine emblem of good fortune that would have appealed to the architects, fitted into the narthex's tympanum. The exterior's pitched roofline proudly carries original finials that have weathered many storms and remain a testament to the waterfront's rich history.

110 Wolcott Street (between Van Brunt and Conover Streets), Brooklyn, NY 11231; 718-625-0103

Part II

Carlmelo Booc.

Sunset Park

Perhaps it was the fact that it was the ideal spot to enjoy the sunset that gave the local park its name. Sunset Park, once considered part of Bay Ridge and still sharing the same postal code, was designated as a separate neighborhood in 1965 and given the official name of its popular park. The region evolved in the 1840s when Irish immigrants arrived, joined by Polish, Norwegian, Swedish and Finnish at the turn of the century. Many were employed on nearby Red Hook docks and others as gardeners and laborers at Green-Wood Cemetery. Bush Terminal, established in 1890, would expand its waterfront depot to more than two hundred acres and provide jobs for thousands of immigrants.

In 1941, the construction of the Gowanus Expressway over 3rd Avenue, as well as its expansion in 1964, cut access to the waterfront and dislocated working families. In the 1950s, when the shipping industry moved to New Jersey, residents also departed, leaving urban decay and unemployment to take over the community. Today, the nearby Bush Terminal piers are slated to be developed as green parks, returning the waterfront to residents, including artists who have discovered affordable lofts. There are more than sixty-seven sacred havens representing the ethnic diversity of the neighborhood, with many retaining original ethnic designations as part of their names. See Bethelship Norwegian United Methodist Church at 5523 4th Avenue, built when Scandinavians were a major segment of the population.

The Sunset Park Recreational Area was mapped out in 1891 to keep the neighborhood from overdevelopment. Once called Dead Man's Hill, the original fourteen acres were expanded to more than twenty-four in 1903 and offer spectacular views of Manhattan, New Jersey and Staten Island. The area as a whole is located between 41st and 44th Streets and between 5th and 7th Avenues.

St. Michael's Roman Catholic Church

The huge Romanesque church just missed the wrecking ball when the area was being revamped in 1903 for the expansion of Sunset Park. Many parishioners' homes were destroyed for the addition and were demolished again in the 1940s for the Gowanus Expressway. The red brick sanctuary, designed by Raymond F. Aimirall, is said to pay homage to Sacré Coeur (Sacred Heart) in Paris. Note the Celtic cross on its cornerstone, a remembrance of Irish immigrants who built the church in 1903. With a distinctive beehive-shaped white dome best seen from Sunset Park, the sanctuary's free-standing two-hundred-foot bell tower dominates the skyline and holds an impressive entrance into the nave. Patron Michael the Archangel sits in a niche above the arched entry, thrusting his spear into the serpentine image of Lucifer, the fallen angel. A decorative interior is filled with round-arched windows, seating for more than one thousand and a lengthy center aisle that is a joy for bridal parties.

352 42nd Street (and 4th Avenue), Brooklyn, NY 11232; 718-768-6065

By the Way

The Parish of St. Rocco was founded in 1902 as a Roman Catholic chapel for Red Hook Italian dockworkers. It moved south in 1914 to the present site, built as the Norwegian Lutheran Church, and has managed to keep the original wrought-iron fence surrounding the exterior that was renovated with a new entrance. In 1956, the church dedicated a youth center on its 4th Avenue corner and remained well known for its student band and outdoor feasts. In the sanctuary, you'll see the image of the twelfth-century patron, who is often invoked for relief from incurable diseases and is accompanied by his faithful canine, which carried food to his sickbed.

216 27th Street (between 4th and 5th Avenues), Brooklyn, NY 11232; 718-768-9798

Iglesia Carismatica Casa de Oracion (4609 8th Avenue) and Iglesia Cristiana La Luz del Mundo (4812 3rd Avenue), which was once an English Lutheran church, are sanctuaries for Hispanic groups, which started to arrive in the 1950s. Along 3rd, 4th and 6th Avenues, there are more than fifteen Hispanic sanctuaries, including Fourth Avenue United Methodist Church (at 4614), housed in a small red brick church with a crenellated corner tower. St. Jacobi Lutheran Church (5406 4th Avenue) was built in 1909 by Norwegians. The Neo-Gothic sanctuary now displays a large banner with the name of its Chinese congregation. Asian immigrants started to settle in the area during the 1980s, establishing their own busy Chinatown on 8th Avenue between 54th and 60th Streets. Also see Grace Chinese Alliance Church at 5633 7th Avenue.

GREEN-WOOD CEMETERY

In 1838, David Bates Douglass was asked by private citizens to design a nonsectarian cemetery for the city of Brooklyn. By 1847, New York State had passed a law forbidding any new burial grounds in Manhattan, causing Brooklyn to boom as a final resting spot. It was also common practice for family remains to be relocated by relatives who were moving into a new area.

Green-Wood became a spiritual place of great beauty with more than 560,000 eternally resting souls within 478 acres. Lessons of history abound with headstones from epidemics, from the Brooklyn Home for Destitute Children when orphans were a major concern for society and from victims of massive fires, including the Brooklyn Theatre Fire in 1876, and the *General Slocum* steamboat disaster in 1904. Civil War general Henry Slocum, for whom the ill-fated ferryboat was named, is also a resident. To see the newest monument on the grounds, walk to Ocean Hill for modern green glass mausoleums topped by twin pyramids sixteen feet tall. They evoke an ancient place of mourning.

Look for Samuel Chester Reid, who got Congress to enact into law the requirement that, upon the admission of a new state, a star would be added to the flag, but the thirteen stripes would remain unchanged (Betsy Ross sewed it for the colonists). His site flies the flag daily. Civil War veterans, estimated at about six thousand, include brothers Clifton and William Prentiss, who fought on opposing sides, were mortally wounded in the same battle and are buried alongside each other. Ten veterans from the Mexican-American War (1846–48) were interred around a granite block marked "Mexico" until individual markers were placed in 2012 to honor each man's sacrifice. Susan

PART II

Smith McKinney-Steward (see Crown Heights), the first African American female physician in New York State, was interred in 1918.

Artisans resting in peace include young modern artist Jean-Michel Basquiat; composer and conductor Leonard Bernstein; and designer Louis Comfort Tiffany and his father, Charles. George Catlin, painter of Native Americans, has an extraordinary bronze sculpture of Chief Black Moccasin near his family plot. Over six feet tall, *The Greeter* was designed and donated in 2011 by John Coleman, who based his image on Catlin's painting of the chief meeting explorers Lewis and Clark at the upper Missouri River. Another impressive character, the Wizard of Oz himself, film actor Frank Morgan, is also resting in perpetuity, as is German chemist Charles Pfizer.

Local Brooklyn hero Charles Ebbets of Ebbets Fields, home of the Dodgers baseball team, is buried near one of his heroes, Henry Chadwick, remembered as the "Father of Baseball." The tall Chadwick monument is topped off with a huge granite baseball and has four stone bases circling its perimeter.

Shady lady Lola Montez (aka Elizabeth Rosanna Gilbert from County Sligo, Ireland) also resides in peaceful bliss. The femme fatale danced her way across Europe, captivating composer Franz Liszt and King Ludwig I of Bavaria, whose indiscretions led to his abdication and to Lola's final journey to New York. In 1998, admirers were lead by Lola's biographer, Bruce Seymour, to dedicate a new headstone. Stop to see *The Bride* watching over Concetta Lupo, who died at twenty-three. The stark, full-length statue is skillfully detailed with a bridal bouquet and lace-patterned gown sculptured by an artisan who must have known her, for love emanates from the stone.

The Gothic Revival landmark entrance gate at 25th Street was designed in 1861 by Richard Upjohn and his son, Richard M., who resides within. A central bell tower is filled with arches, spires and carvings, as well as a clock to remind all of passing time. Inside on Battle Hill, the Greek goddess Minerva stands with an outstretched arm seemingly to greet the Statue of Liberty, which can be seen in New York Harbor. Minerva commemorates the Battle of Brooklyn and the fallen soldiers of the Maryland Brigade (see the Stone House in Park Slope).

Be sure to visit the historic English Gothic chapel, which can seat 120 and whose oak-fitted interior was restored in 1999. It was designed in 1911 by Warren & Wetmore, famous for Manhattan's Grand Central Terminal, and includes fine windows by William Willet. It is open daily whenever the cemetery gates are open.

500 25th Street, Brooklyn, NY 11232; 718-768-7300

CHURCH OF OUR LADY OF CZESTOCHOWA–ST. CASIMIR

Polish congregations have always held sacred one of Christianity's oldest icons, the Black Madonna. Its legend is filled with miraculous events, stories of survival through great tragedies, and it symbolizes the indestructibility of Poland's faith during the ruthless World War II German invasion. The icon of Mary as the Black Madonna is said to have been found in Jerusalem by St. Helen in AD 326 and given to her son, Constantine, emperor of the Byzantine-Roman empire. It arrived in Poland through a royal dowry and then to Czestochowa during a war in 1382. The icon was attacked in 1430, and those slashes remain on Mary's face and in all reproductions.

In 1896, this parish was begun as a mission of St. Casimir's Church, founded in 1875 by Polish immigrants (see Paul Robeson Theater entry). St. John the Evangelist (at 250 21st Street), which was opened in 1849, was the only Roman Catholic sanctuary in the neighborhood, but since rituals were celebrated in English, there was a need to care for immigrants arriving without benefit of the language. In 1980, the founding community from Fort Greene united with its mission chapel on the present site that once held a Lutheran church.

Our Lady of Czestochowa.

Architect John Ryan designed the red brick Gothic church in 1904 and is remembered in the stained-glass window of St. John the Evangelist. An intimate interior, sitting five hundred, has a hand-carved wooden altar made in Poland and an elaborate reredos filled with delicate spires and polychrome statues tucked into niches. It is here that the gilded image of the Black Madonna is honored with an icon painted by the Pauline fathers in Poland. Under the portrait, two free-standing angels hold shields that read *Pokoj* ("peace") and *Milosc* ("love").

Stained-glass images of saints revered by the community surround the vaulted nave, including Casimir (1458–1482), who is the patron of Poland and son of a king. While suffering from tuberculosis, Casimir became devoted to the mother of Jesus during his short life and is remembered in the "Hymn of St. Casimir," a recitation in Mary's honor.

Be sure to stop by the shrine of Blessed Maximilian Kolbe, a Polish priest who perished at Auschwitz when he took the place of a Jewish family man. Also look for the copper wall plaque honoring Pope John Paul II, the pride of the Polish community worldwide. A bronze statue of the pope in flowing robes and mitered headdress stands outside the rectory on 25th Street. The congregation celebrates rituals in both English and Polish and shares cultural traditions in the parish center, named for founding pastor Reverend Boleslaus Puchalski, who served the congregation more than sixty years until his death.

183 25th Street (between 3rd and 4th Avenues), Brooklyn, NY 11232; 718-768-5724

OUR LADY OF PERPETUAL HELP

In 1893, a temporary frame church was opened on the present property by a far-sighted congregation that dedicated at the same time a marble cornerstone for a grander edifice. The summer community's sanctuary evolved into Brooklyn's largest Roman Catholic church, with schools and a rectory that fill an entire city block. The grand entrance was planned on fashionable 5th Avenue, while the *Brooklyn Daily Eagle* newspaper described the sanctuary as "the little church on the hill, a church on the edge of the fields." Trolley cars, leading south to Fort Hamilton, were introduced along 5th Avenue in 1896, and two years later, the city of Brooklyn merged with New York. After the large Kent estate was sold, row houses were developed that attracted permanent residents along with transient summer visitors.

Mural in Our Lady of Perpetual Help.

In 1909, Reverend John B. Daily of the Redemptorist Fathers helped the German and Irish congregation of five thousand to open a lower church, but they would not start the upper church until they were debt-free. Meanwhile, the new 4th Avenue subway brought easier access to the area, and in 1925, another cornerstone was dedicated, with services held in the unfinished upper sanctuary in 1928.

Architect Thomas F. Houghton designed the huge Neo-Romanesque Revival granite church, which reaches more than 100 feet high, with a front porch. It has a bilateral entry to access the upper and lower church, with each level seating 1,800 worshipers. The interior's round archways support clerestory stained-glass windows that line the 258-foot-long cruciform sanctuary. Stone walls from Bath, England, hold medieval-like stained glass, while Stations of the Cross are fashioned in Italian mosaics. Look up to the dome's glorious mural of Mary, the mother of Jesus, ascending to heaven with crowds of apostles below and heavenly hosts on high.

A lavish side altar, dedicated in 1933 to the patron as Our Lady of Perpetual Help, displays Mary's gilded portrait with the infant Jesus, who is guarded by two life-size angels under a deep blue mosaic dome filled with golden stars. The shrine was designed by Maginnis and Walsh, which utilized onyx wainscoting and tangerine-stained stone on the altar façade. Written within golden mosaics, "Behold Thy Mother" are thoughtful words from the dying Jesus to his apostle John, entrusting Mary to his care.

Because of the church's size, many diocesan celebrations are held in the upper sanctuary, while the lower sanctuary is opened for daily services. In 2003, when Nicholas A. DiMarzio Jr. was appointed the seventh bishop, he was formally presented here to the people of Brooklyn, and he continues to hold ceremonies within this grand place of worship. Services are celebrated in English, Chinese, Spanish and Vietnamese, along with colorful images of both the Guadalupe and Cuban Madonnas, as well as the crucified Christ from Columbia.

526 59ᵗʰ Street (between 5ᵗʰ and 6ᵗʰ Avenues), Brooklyn, NY 11220; 718-492-9200

FATIH CAMII (FATIH MOSQUE)

Tucked into busy Chinatown, this Turkish-styled mosque was opened in 1980 on a site that had been both movie theater and Norwegian dance club. The golden-brick two-story building is now a large sanctuary, with

Fatih Mosque prayer room.

interior walls covered in serene blue and white tiles. Since the use of figurative design is forbidden, all motifs are done in geometric patterns. In this orthodox tradition, men and women worship separately and remove footwear before entering the blue-carpeted prayer room. The imam, leader of the congregation, conducts the service from the minbar, or pulpit. Look for the mihrab, the tiled niche representing the presence of the Prophet Muhammad; it points toward Mecca, the Saudi Arabian city that holds the ancient Kaaba shrine in the Grand Mosque.

The United American Muslim Association of New York is headquartered here and sponsors two other mosques in the neighborhood: Fatih Talebe Yurdu at 813 60th Street and Sunset Kiz Yurdu at 863 59th Street.

5911 8th Avenue (at 59th Street), Brooklyn, NY 11220; 718-438-6919

BY THE WAY

Grace Baptist Church welcomes English, Spanish, Chinese and Russian members and prides itself on its multicultural services. The congregation was founded in 1886 as West End Baptist Church and merged with the 4th Avenue Baptist Church to build this large Neo-Gothic sanctuary. Dedicated in 1914, the intimate interior has seating for five hundred, a baptismal pool and one main aisle.

5224 6th Avenue (and 53rd Street), Brooklyn, NY 11220; 718-492-4141

Second Evangelical Free Church dedicated its cornerstone in 1913 for the yellow-brick Gothic Church that now sits in Chinatown. Its designation retains the word "free" as a reminder that pews were once rented, a major disadvantage to newly arriving immigrants. The Christian congregation welcomes all ethnic groups into its diverse community.

5201 8th Avenue, Brooklyn, NY 11220; 718-436-0716

Bay Ridge and Fort Hamilton

The rural region only developed at the beginning of the twentieth century when wealthy New Yorkers began to build summer mansions overlooking the harbor. Bay Ridge, named for the glacial ridge left by the last ice age, once covered a large area that made it a strategic site during the colonial rebellion of 1776. The American Revolution War Cemetery, also known as the Barkaloo Cemetery for the Dutch family whose two sons were war victims, still sits on the corner of Narrows Avenue and MacKay Place. Legend says that the plot holds about fifty citizens, including soldiers who died during the Battle of Brooklyn. Owl's Head Park, the thirty-acre site at Shore Road between 68th Street and Colonial Road, once belonged to the powerful lawyer Henry C. Murphy, who helped plan the Brooklyn Bridge. In 1915, the 4th Avenue subway line opened, and the building boom began.

Fort Hamilton was built in 1814 in response to the burning of Washington, D.C., during the War of 1812. Named for the first U.S. secretary of the treasury, Alexander Hamilton, the fort guarded the Narrows between Brooklyn and Staten Island and remains on active duty. Harbor Defense Museum, once the storehouse for the post, is full of military souvenirs and has a self-guided walking tour available (718-630-4349).

During the 1870s, large numbers of Norwegian, Swedish and Danish sailors began settling in the area while working in the shipping industry. Norwegians are still here, joined by Irish, Italian, Greek, Hispanic, Asian, Arab and other ethnic groups. Situated among the many sacred havens, older mansions and brick homes dramatically contrast with modern residential buildings.

VERRAZANO-NARROWS BRIDGE

Spanning more than 4,200 feet, this suspension bridge made its debut in November 1964. It is named for Italian navigator Giovanni da Verrazzano, who led an expedition to the northeastern coast of North America in 1524 and was the first European known to sail into New York Harbor, under the French flag.

Designed by Othmar H. Ammann (who also designed the George Washington Bridge in 1931), the bridge reaches 623 feet in height and features a two-level roadway but lacks a pedestrian path. Today, ships still pass through the narrowest part of New York Harbor but now under the bridge anchored in Brooklyn's Fort Hamilton and Staten Island's Fort Wadsworth. The project was restarted by the "master builder," Robert Moses, chairman of the Triborough Bridge and Tunnel Authority; it had been a dream of the agency for more than eighty years. Since more than eight thousand residents would be displaced, opposition was intense, but Staten Island boomed as Brooklyn families moved over the bridge to greener pastures.

Verrazano-Narrows Bridge in Fort Hamilton.

St. John's Episcopal Church
(Church of the Generals)

Government officials in stained glass: St. Matthew, the former tax collector, and Abraham Lincoln, former president of the United States, at St. John's Episcopal Church.

When this church was founded in 1834, the bucolic village of Fort Hamilton communicated via its daily stagecoach trip to Flatbush, then on to Manhattan. The site, part of the Denyse Farm, which included most of Fort Hamilton, was donated by the Denyse family, and the sanctuary built in just one year. Since most of the congregation was from the garrison, a uniformed band led the church's dedication procession. Records indicate that the parish was devastated by an outbreak of yellow fever in 1875 and was closed for two years.

Because membership has included officers from the Mexican-American War in the 1840s up to the Vietnam War in the 1960s, the sanctuary is affectionately called "Church of the Generals." The church's vestryman and the fort's engineer in 1840, General Robert E. Lee, led the southern Confederate troops in the Civil War but not before he planted a tree in the front yard. Thomas "Stonewall" Jackson, baptized here as an adult in 1849, earned his nickname at Manassass during the Civil War and also led Confederate troops in the Shenandoah Valley Campaign. Henry Slocum, a Northern Civil War hero, is remembered for an ill-equipped ferryboat bearing his name that sank in the East River on June 1905; the incident was the worst maritime disaster in United States history, claiming more than one thousand lives. See General Slocum's window commemorating the Georgia regiment. Others remembered are General Matthew Ridgway, who led the U.S. forces during the Korean War; General Walter Bedell Smith, chief of staff to General Dwight D. Eisenhower during World War II; and U.S. Air Force general Hubert Harmon, the first superintendent of the U.S. Air Force Academy.

In 1966, a disastrous fire destroyed the church's interior, but the congregation skillfully rebuilt its sanctuary by accepting furnishings from other churches and extending the nave's floor plan. The flagstone complex is clustered on a corner lot, and its exterior, encircled by a wrought-iron fence and garden, holds a vivid polychrome crucifix of Christ with his mother, Mary, and Patron John the Evangelist. A small narthex remains filled with stained glass detailing the sacraments, including matrimony and baptism.

Walk into an intimate nave with black-and-white floor tiles; it seats about 150 worshipers and is divided between the old and newer section restored after the fire. Decorative wood rafters support the *Great Rood*, while a golden triptych similar to Orthodox icons and a brass lectern faced with the American eagle enhance the apse. Original stained-glass windows line the front walls of the nave, while the back of the sanctuary holds the baptismal font, whose plaque honors "Stonewall" Jackson. The new wall of clear glass with colorful images is glorious. Twenty-four leaded images are creatively paired as historical figures: writers St. Mark and C.S. Lewis; defenders of freedom St. Philip and Dr. Martin Luther King; and government officials St. Matthew, the former tax collector, and Abraham Lincoln. While Fort Hamilton continues operating as a military base, and St. John's rector still serves as a chaplain, this haven now stands in the shadow of the Verrazano-Narrows Bridge entrance ramps; it became a more modern way to communicate with Staten Island.

9818 Fort Hamilton Parkway (and 99th Street), Brooklyn, NY 11209; 718-745-2377

ST. PATRICK'S ROMAN CATHOLIC CHURCH

In 1849, Reverend Peter McLoughlin started the chapel of St. Patrick for Catholic soldiers assigned to Fort Hamilton. Along with farmers and fishermen, the fort's enlisted men generously contributed to build a wooden sanctuary, which was dedicated in 1852 by Bishop John Hughes from Manhattan. He was rowed across the Narrows from Staten Island. In 1853, Bay Ridge boundaries were set, and the village of Fort Hamilton was established along the shore, but the area would remain isolated until the Brooklyn Bridge opened in 1883 and the Brooklyn Elevated Railroad began running in 1885.

Ferry service to Staten Island started at 69th Street in Bay Ridge in 1912, but when the subway opened to 86th Street in 1916 and extended to 95th Street in 1923, it would have the greater impact on the community. Rapid increase in population established new parishes but also encouraged the need for St. Patrick's to build a new church in 1926. Today's large light brick Italianate church with the asymmetrical tower reflected not only the parish growth but also its anticipation of future settlers.

The portico, with a limestone arcade and tripartite entry, leads into the narthex filled with a wall of clear leaded glass set into wood panels to separate it from the nave. Look over the middle door for the white-bearded image of the patron with his bishop's miter and crosier, along with the three-leaf shamrock that Patrick used to explain the doctrine of the Trinity.

Polychrome, three-dimensional Stations of the Cross are placed at eye level beneath stained-glass windows lining the open nave, while a softly colored mosaic of the Crucifixion encased in a round arch is the focus of the apse. The church continues to witness the neighborhood's evolution and to hold services for the army base, just like the old days.

9511 4th Avenue (and 95th Street), Brooklyn, NY 11209; 718-238-2600

NARROWS BOTANICAL GARDENS

Belt Parkway parallels over four acres of gardens where you can enjoy views of the Verrazano Bridge, the Statue of Liberty and the Narrows without obstruction. Volunteers turned once neglected space into a living gift for neighbors to enjoy concerts, harbor ships and regal roses. See the Native Plant Garden, Turtle Sanctuary and the Rock Wall among its offerings. Lucky students from Xaverian High School, built in 1960 at 71st Street, are directly across the road. The garden receives no government funding and is located on Shore Road between 69th and 72nd Streets. Volunteers and new members can contact www.narrowsbg.org or write to 7304 5th Avenue, PO Box 242, Brooklyn, New York, 11209.

HOLY CROSS GREEK ORTHODOX CHURCH

The parish was incorporated in 1957 by seven men who saw not only a need for a church but also a way to preserve their Hellenic culture. After several moves, the congregation purchased the present site and built its traditional church designed by W. Chiagotis. Parish records indicate how grateful the members were to Union Church for allowing them to worship in the Union facilities until their new home opened in 1966.

Interior of Holy Cross Greek Orthodox Church.

This peach-colored brick and limestone Byzantine church sits regally atop a corner garden surrounded by black wrought-iron fencing. An entry porch with three rounded arches supported by white wood columns and an asymmetrical tower complete the façade. Look for golden mosaic artwork dominating the main entry: the icon of Christ crucified and images of Mary and John the Evangelist placed above side doors.

The white marbled narthex, with icons of St. Nicholas and St. Helen with her son, Constantine, prepares you to enter the nave filled with decorative sacred images. An interior dome features *Christ Pantocrator* (*Great High Priest*), while the marble iconostatis holds icons revered by the congregation and sacred entry doors used by the clergy. A colorful mural of *The Last Supper* adorns the balcony's façade, while stained-glass windows display individual saintly images. See Nicholas, beloved saint in eastern and western Christianity, standing within bright yellow stained glass.

8401 Ridge Boulevard (between 4ᵗʰ and 85ᵗʰ Streets), Brooklyn, NY 11209; 718-836-3510

Union Church of Bay Ridge

Church archives report that before there were bridges or subways, there was a congregation worshiping on this site. In 1896, it was home to the Dutch Reformed Church, which merged in 1918 with the Presbyterian church on 81st Street. Hence, its name recognized the official union. When the sanctuary opened, Tiffany's window *The Resurrection of Christ*, with a glistening white-robed Jesus surrounded by Mary Magdalene and angels at his tomb, was installed. It is dedicated to Rulef Van Brunt (1823–1883), who donated the land for the building.

In 1924, the present structure was extended to the east, with thirteen stained-glass windows added; the addition included *Angel of the Resurrection* by Louis Lederle, which was placed in the chancel above a dark wood altar screen trimmed with carved pinnacles. The clerestory's nine windows were English imports, each featuring an angel extolling symbols of Christian virtue. Look for *Praise* and *Prayer* with memorial inscriptions and be sure to see the baptismal font and sacramental table fashioned in rich wood. The last

Union Church of Bay Ridge.

clerestory window, *Mine Eyes Have Seen the Glory*, was installed as a memorial in 1980 for Peter Wilhousky (1902–1972), music director and arranger of "The Battle Hymn of the Republic." His window features an early Christian family gazing up to the anthem's title imprinted on a banner.

When the church's tower was destroyed by lightning in 1934, this low stone building with terra-cotta trim was redesigned at its corner site. A crenellated roofline added panache to the double entryway that also held the cornerstone from 1896.

8101 Ridge Boulevard (and 80ᵗʰ Street), Brooklyn, NY 11209; 718-745-0438

ST. ANSELM CHURCH

Since the neighborhood began to expand rapidly due to the subway's arrival in 1915, some Roman Catholics began holding services in 1922 at the Fitzgerald family residence until their first church could be completed on the present site. Today, that building is used as an auditorium, while the red brick and stone church designed by Henry V. Murphy in 1953 remains a testimony to the congregation's vision.

An impressive Art Deco exterior holds a wheel window encircled with marble and featuring a limestone image of the Holy Spirit as a dove. Beneath the window, rose marble panels engraved in Latin tell of the Holy Spirit's seven gifts: *sapientia* (wisdom), *intellectus* (understanding), *consilium* (the spirit of counsel), *fortitudo* (strength), *scientia* (the spirit of knowledge), *pietas* (piety) and *timor* (fear of the Lord). Three bronze entry doors are guarded by warrior angels, while the octagonal bell tower's façade is home to even more angelic hosts.

The long, narrow interior with a single center aisle holds stylized stained-glass windows depicting scenes from Genesis to Pentecost. Look for Adam and Eve in the flourishing Garden of Eden, with the white-maned image of God peering down at them. The interior, designed by Lief Neandross of the Rambusch Company, features Patron Anselm in a golden mosaic surrounded by an embossed white arch on the reredos. The bronze baldachin in the rose marble apse also directs your eye upward to a colorful mural filled with events in the life of Jesus.

Anselm (1033–1109) was born a nobleman in Piedmont, entered into monastic life and spoke against the injustices of King William Rufus as archbishop of Canterbury. Having to leave England, he became a defender of the Church against the usurpation of kings and returned to Rome, where his ontological argument for the existence of God strongly influenced philosophers and theologians. Celebrated as "Doctor of the Church," Anselm's coat of arms and an image of the Canterbury Cathedral has been included on the reredos.

356 82nd Street (and 4th Avenue), Brooklyn, NY 11209; 718-238-2900

Good Shepherd Evangelical Lutheran Church

In 1906, twenty-three neighbors, headed by Pastor Charles D. Trexler, gathered for worship in Firemen's Hall on Bay Ridge Avenue and also began a Sunday school for nineteen children. They were a mixed group of immigrants, unlike most congregations that were designated by specific ethnicities. Property was purchased, and three years later, the group acquired the vacant Christ Episcopal Church, built in 1853 at 3rd Avenue and 68th Street. It moved the building to the present site and held its first service in 1910.

A gray stucco exterior, with multiple gables and steeples adding to its charm, is anchored by a corner tower with a copper steeple. Highlighted by a front garden that borders the façade's Gothic-arched windows, the building is further enhanced by red doors at two entrances. A small projecting porch reminds you of the light that is always left on to guide neighbors in the darkness, much like the teachings of Martin Luther, who led the Reformation movement. The Augsberg Confession that Luther wrote with Philp Melanchton in 1530 was meant to reform practices within the Roman Catholic Church but instead led to the formation of the Lutheran sect.

7420 4th Avenue (and 75th Street), Brooklyn, NY 11209; 718-745-8520

Our Lady of Angels Roman Catholic Church

The congregation held its first Mass during 1891 in a firehouse on 67th Street between 2nd and 3rd Avenues. Records show that public facility managers were very receptive to neighbors who needed space for gatherings. The community grew to build its first church on this site in 1893 and the present church in 1929. Massive red brick and limestone building has Patron Mary's

Our Lady of Angels.

image sculptured on the tympanum that is engraved, "S. Maria Angelorum Dicatum" (dedicated to "Mary, Queen of the Angels"). The impressive portal is faced with Corinthian columns supporting Art Deco angels, while a round window filled with tracery and a vertical row of thirteen vacant niches adorn the upper façade.

The serene cruciform interior has marble shrines in the transepts, each with a rose window adding colorful light. Green, cream and tangerine marble columns line the nave's walls and act as buttresses between stained-glass windows whose designs resemble pages from medieval Bibles. Look for Peter commemorated as the first pope. The focus of the wide-open sanctuary is the mural of Mary within the green marble-columned apse, which also has a soundproof "crying room" tucked into one side for young families in the congregation. As you sit in the oak pews among the many angels, golden capitals and coffered ceiling, there is a sense of peace that cannot be disturbed even after you feel the subway rumbling beneath your feet.

7320 4ᵗʰ Avenue (and 73ʳᵈ Street), Brooklyn, NY 11209; 718-836-7200

Part II

Fourth Avenue Presbyterian Church

This Neo-Gothic red brick church was built in 1957 and has an interesting history. Syrian Christian immigrants who wanted to worship in their Arabic language and with their liturgy and ritual incorporated in 1907 as the Syrian Protestant Church. The group first met in rented spaces and found a home in 1920 on Clinton and Pacific Streets. In the 1940s, the members began English services and joined the Presbyterian sect under the leadership of Reverend Edward Jurji. The congregation then relocated to Bay Ridge, constructed the present sanctuary "with the labor of its own members" and continued to grow.

The sanctuary's rectangular interior, with exposed wooden rafters, has one main aisle leading to the apse. It focuses on a huge dark wooden cross that hangs on an unadorned wall above a white marble altar table. Traditional stained-glass windows line the side aisles, while in back of the sanctuary, a huge window entitled *Our Father Who Art in Heaven* shows throngs of followers looking up to Jesus, who is surrounded by a multitude of angels. Dedicated to the memory of Habib Merhige and Amin Merhige, the window is detailed with hills, trees and foliage reminiscent of the Middle East. Membership evolved to include worshipers from many nations, but its Arabic roots have not been forgotten.

6753 4ᵗʰ Avenue (between Senator and 68ᵗʰ Streets), Brooklyn, NY 11220; 718-836-0681

Leif Ericson Park

A narrow stretch of 1.65 acres lines the avenue and holds a significant monument dedicated to Leif Ericson (circa 960–circa 1020), who is said to have discovered America in the year AD 1000. Since Norwegians were a huge segment of the population, they would be honored by Crown Prince Olav of Norway, who dedicated this tribute on July 6, 1939. It is a replica of a rune stone that traditionally honors Viking heroes. A brass plaque of a fashionable Viking (helmet, shield, spear and ship) tells the explorer's story. Leif Ericson

Viking plaque in Leif Ericson Park.

Day was declared by President Lyndon B. Johnson's proclamation on October 9, 1964, but the annual crowning of Miss Norway takes place in May during the Norwegian Constitution Day Parade. Located at 4th Avenue between 66th and 67th Streets, the park's tribute to Ericson is on the triangle east of 4th Avenue.

BY THE WAY

Property records of Bay Ridge Baptist Church show that there has been a church on this site from the late 1800s. Today's beige, stucco, one-story building dates from 1952 and, like all Baptist congregations, is managed independently. Brown accents trim the façade, while the round archway surrounds an entry with red doors. The sanctuary's unadorned interior, with wood wainscoting, features the pastor's pulpit in the apse along with the baptismal pool.

6701 4th Avenue (and 67th Street), Brooklyn, NY 11209; 718-238-0555

The Islamic Society of Bay Ridge built an unassuming mosque in 2000 after Middle Easterners moved to Bay Ridge in the early 1990s. It is surrounded by retail stores, halal butcher shops and restaurants, as well as schools for Moslem children and adults. Since prayer is required five times a day, there is always traffic on the avenue. Nearby Sunset Park has three mosques for those working or visiting the area.

6807 5th Avenue (and 68th Street), Brooklyn, NY 11220; 718-680-0121

Dyker Heights

With a huge golf course and park on Gravesend Bay, Dyker Heights was once part of Bay Ridge, and many residents still claim it as their neighborhood. Generations of Italian families have lived here in private homes, while more than ten Christian havens tell of the many sects that also settled in the area.

ST. EPHREM ROMAN CATHOLIC CHURCH

The first sanctuary was founded in 1921 by Reverend Richard A. Kennedy and became the schoolbuilding after the present haven was constructed in 1953 in front of the property. During the early 1960s, construction of Interstate 287 destroyed hundreds of homes and positioned the church to face the roadway.

Designed by Paul C. Reilly, the red brick Georgian building with a slate roof has an arched portico and garden extending around its corner site. The white interior is reminiscent of Colonial Williamsburg, with mahogany wainscoting, brass lighting fixtures and fluted columns with golden capitals. A gilded marble baldachin on the altar is supported by slim, veined-marble columns and displays Ephrem's crest. Be sure to look in the choir loft for an ornate plaster grill adding interesting wall texture.

Tall, glorious leaded windows, created by Joeb Nicolas of the Rambusch Company, who designed the interior, feature figurative center panels painted

Colonial Interior of St. Ephrem.

on milk-white glass. They tell traditional biblical stories: Adam and Eve being ejected from the Garden of Eden, John baptizing Jesus and the apostles gathered at the Last Supper.

Patron Ephrem of Syria was born in the fourth century under Roman rule. After converting to Christianity, he fled persecution and became famous for his sermons and prayers written in poetic verse. Known as the "Harp of the Holy Spirit" for introducing hymns into worship, Ephrem can be seen in the gilded Orthodox icon by Benjamin D'Arconte (1933–2003). Be sure to stop by the exterior memorial for the nine parishioners killed on 9/11—the bronze statue of a kneeling Jesus cradles the Twin Towers—and the heartfelt quotation from Isaiah 49 that reads, "I will never forget you, see upon the palm of my hands I have written your name. Your walls are ever before me."

929 Bay Ridge Parkway (between Fort Hamilton Pkwy and 10th Avenue at 74th Street), Brooklyn, NY 11228; 718-833-1010

St. Frances Cabrini

The Second Ecumenical Council of the Vatican in 1963, under Pope Paul VI (successor to Pope John XXIII who started the modernization process of Roman Catholic liturgy), was an impetus for Thomas Cardinal Daily to start a new parish and also relieve the overcrowded pews at St. Finbar's in Bensonhurst.

Reverends Anthony J. Ryder and Charles P. Boccio borrowed an altar from St. Finbar's and held the first Mass on the present site. In the fall, the group moved indoors to an auto showroom, then to Scarpaci Funeral Home and on to the Knights of Columbus Hall while waiting for the church.

In 1967, this modern underground brick sanctuary was dedicated to a modern woman with quite a record of achievements. Mother Frances Cabrini (1850–1917), who had founded a religious order of teachers, arrived in New York City from Italy in 1883 to start schools, hospitals, orphanages and nursing homes, specifically for Italian immigrants who were living in deplorable conditions. Frances had wanted to serve in China, but her mission was decided by Pope Leo XIII, who was aware of the Italian American problem.

An exterior steeple, with an open bell tower, rises to form a cross above the façade, while St. Francis Cabrini's statue is tucked above the main entry. Glass windows hold no images, only engraved names of donors and deceased parishioners. In the underground sanctuary, a simple altar table is placed within a shallow, wood-paneled apse that also holds a polychrome sculpture of the patron in her traditional black habit. Nearby, a votive chapel features icons dear to the community.

1562 86th Street (and 16th Avenue), Brooklyn, NY 11228; 718-236-9165

St. George Coptic Orthodox Church

The evangelist Mark is said to have established the first Egyptian Christian church in AD 42, with the Copts identified as original Egyptian descendants of that ancient church. Their pope holds the seat of the Coptic Orthodox church, which was begun during the sixth century in Alexandria in reaction to theological disputes with Greek Orthodox administrators. Both groups have managed to exist as minorities among legions of Moslems and Islamic extremists.

St. George Coptic Orthodox Church.

In 1972, the Neo-Romanesque red brick Baptist church built in 1928 was purchased by the Middle East congregation. The group expanded the building in 1984, and again in 1996, to seat more than five hundred members, who travel from all five boroughs.

An enormous bronze metal image of Patron George sits above the single entry that has Coptic crosses carved into wooden doors. The cross is of two equal lengths, with three points at each angle representing the Trinity—twelve points in all honoring the apostles, who spread the gospel. An iconic image of *Christ Pantocrator* (*Great High Priest*) accompanied by two lively angels is featured on the corner façade. Perhaps one day, the rooftop's white cupola will become a Byzantine dome, a missing element in the interior that features handsome icons and crystal chandeliers.

With continuing attacks on Egyptian Copts, the congregation has witnessed enormous growth since 2010, a sad reminder of earlier immigrants who arrived under similar circumstances.

1105 67ʰ Street (and 11ʰ Avenue), Brooklyn, NY 11219; 718-259-1564

Part II

St. Rosalie–Regina Pacis Parish

The Parish of St. Rosalie was founded in 1902 by Italian immigrants who named their new venture after the patron saint of Palermo, Sicily. In May 1942, the congregation made a pledge to Mary, the mother of Jesus, to build a shrine after the safe return of their World War II soldiers and to continue to pray for peace. Hence, the two sacred havens would be considered one parish.

St. Rosalie's beige stucco Neo-Gothic exterior, with a simple portico supported by white columns, reflects early immigrant founders. Regina Pacis ("Queen of Peace") would become a tribute to the next generation of Italian families who prospered in America and generously financed their new shrine. In 1951, several blocks away from St. Rosalie, the congregation dedicated this huge Italian Renaissance sanctuary designed by Anthony J. Depace with a Latin inscription on the limestone façade's lintel that notes its purpose, "in fulfillment of a vow."

Artifacts of great beauty fill the interior, whose threshold is inlaid with the words "In Viam Pacis" ("On Your Way to Peace"). The nave rises more than fifty-seven feet and is more than sixty-three feet wide. Magnificent clerestory

Regina Pacis Sanctuary.

windows by the Edward W. Hiemer Studios, thirty types of marble, six side chapels and Mary's life story in ceiling murals by Ignacio LaRussa are among the inspirational offerings to visitors.

In the coffered-ceiling apse, a marble throne rising more than thirty-four feet holds an onyx-framed portrait by Ilario Panzironi of Regina Pacis—Mary holding her young son, Jesus, who waves a generous olive branch in his tiny hand—and putti (angels) featured in heavenly clouds. On the arch surrounding the choir loft, angels play bells and sing hymns, while the colorfully garbed archangel Michael greets visitors in the narthex. Be sure to walk the nave's ambulatory to see fourteen mosaic images of the Stations of the Cross, each having carved stone frames inlaid with red marble. Luisi Eredi from Pietrasanta, Italy, was responsible for the outstanding marble work throughout the entire building. The congregation clearly endowed the neighborhood with a lasting gift and a reminder of the never-ending quest for peace.

St. Rosalie Church, 6301 14th Avenue (at 64th Street), and the Shrine of Regina Pacis, 1260 65th Street (at 12th Avenue); parish office is at 718-236-0909

BY THE WAY

Additional sanctuaries from early settlers remain: Redeemer St. John's Lutheran Church at 939 83rd Street; St. Philip's Episcopal Church, on its original site from 1900, at 1072 80th Street; and six Roman Catholic churches, including the Shrine of St. Bernadette from 1935 at 8201 13th Avenue and Our Lady of Guadalupe, with its red tile roof, founded in 1906 at 7201 15th Avenue.

Bensonhurst and Bath Beach

Bath Beach, named for the spa town of Bath, England, is part of Bensonhurst, originally the Benson Farm in the Dutch settlement of New Utrecht. As neighborhoods developed, the former name of New Utrecht was replaced, but it still survives on sacred havens and street signs.

When the Revolutionary War was ending in 1783, colonists erected a liberty pole and began the custom of flying an American flag. Traditions of early Italian settlers from Sicily are also thriving among descendants, who still reside in private homes and are proprietors of the bustling shopping area on 18th Avenue and 86th Street. Bensonhurst Park, a pleasant spot to rest your spirit, continues for three miles along Belt Parkway. It's located at 21st Avenue and Bay Parkway. There are more than sixteen churches in the area, while a large Jewish population that is heavily composed of Middle Eastern Sephardic immigrants has more than fourteen synagogues. The Jewish Community House of Bensonhurst at 7802 Bay Parkway offers educational and cultural programs.

New Utrecht Reformed Church

This landmark granite church marks the site where the village of New Utrecht was founded in 1661. The first church was probably constructed after Peter Stuyvesant, the sixth and last director-general, ordered the Flatbush Dutch Reformed Church (see entry) to be built in 1655. Ministers arrived from the Netherlands, firmly rooted in the Reformed Church of Holland, and ushered into the New World the oldest Protestant church in America, with its creed relying on scriptures and its administration on elders and deacons. As populations increased, several ministers alternated traveling to communities, thus beginning the first collegiate, or colleague system, of a shared ministry. The term "collegiate" still exists in several Manhattan churches.

Dutch governance ended in 1664, but King William III of England, who was of Dutch ancestry, granted a full charter to the Dutch Reformed Church in 1696, firmly establishing its right in the British colony of New York. The British occupied Brooklyn from August 1776 to November 1783 and used this property as a hospital and a riding school.

Today, the large site, enclosed within black fencing, holds the 1828 church that was fashioned from the original building's stones. It is charmingly symmetrical, with white-framed Gothic windows and a small, circular Federal-style window above bright red doors. Side walls are lined with tinted windows, while vestiges of former entrances remain without staircases. On the back of the property, a Neo-Romanesque red brick parish house was erected in 1892, with entrance doors in its squat tower.

It was on this site in 1783 that colonists, wishing to display their flag of independence, invented the liberty pole (replaced many times). Still on display, look up to see its antique weathervane, with "LIBERTY" emblazoned on the directional arrow and an original wooden eagle spanning its wings.

1827 84th Street (at 18th Avenue), Brooklyn, NY 11214; 718-236-0678

New Utrecht
Reformed
Church.

ST. FINBAR ROMAN CATHOLIC CHURCH

Estates and holiday resorts brought many visitors to the Bath Beach and Gravesend Bay area when this church was founded in 1880. Prosperous resident William Swayne offered land to Bishop John Loughlin if the bishop would build a church named for the first bishop of Cork City in southern Ireland. Patron Finbar (550–633) founded a monastery in the seventh century that became a European center of learning.

The original wood-frame church was only one room and was built when the nativist movement was still popular in New York City. Roman Catholic immigrants were considered inferior to Anglo-Saxon Protestant groups, and many Catholic churches were destroyed by fire. But far removed in this suburban area, St. Finbar's congregation felt safe enough to worship freely and opened a parish school in 1889, attesting to its growth. By 1910, a cornerstone had been dedicated for this larger haven.

During this decade, the Church of St. Athanasius was founded in 1913, at 2154 61st Street, for Italian immigrants from Williamsburg and Manhattan's Lower East Side, but they would continue to relocate down south to this greener environment. St. Finbar's never ceased growing and became the largest congregation in Brooklyn. By 1963, another parish was deemed necessary, and St. Frances Cabrini was opened in Dyker Heights (see entry).

The light brick Italian Renaissance church has a cruciform interior with barrel vaulted ceilings and marblelike columns. Decorative murals that cover the walls and ceiling in the 180-foot-long interior are from Italian artists, while figurative windows were imported from Germany. Look in stained glass for Patron Finbar in his bishop's robes, as well as small images of his monastery and the miter (headdress) and crosier (pastoral staff).

138 Bay 20th Street (between Bath and Benson), Brooklyn, NY 11214; 718-236-3312

MAGEN DAVID CONGREGATION

In the early 1900s, Syrian immigrants belonging to many sects began arriving on Manhattan's Lower East Side. Syrian Jews from Damascus and Aleppo moved across the Williamsburg Bridge and eventually south to this neighborhood. Because of political unrest in recent years, Middle Eastern immigration has increased dramatically, and Jews from Lebanon, Egypt, Morroco, Israel, Iran and Iraq have taken up residency.

The landmark synagogue was founded by Syrians in 1920 and is now utilized for funeral services because of limited seating for two hundred. The Orthodox congregation follows Sephardic (Hebrew for Spain) tradition. The Torah is read from the bema, placed in the center of the sanctuary, and men and women worship in segregated sections. The large community of Syrian Jews overflowed to Ocean Parkway, where members built grander synagogues for the community.

2028 66th Street (at 20th Avenue), Brooklyn, NY 11214; 718-236-6122

By the Way

Since walking distance is important, all synagogues are centered near family homes. Other havens include Beth Hatalmud, dedicated in 1948 at 2127 82nd Street (718-259-2525), and Tifereth Torah of Bensonhurst at 8224 23rd Avenue and 83rd Street (718-236-6646).

Congregation Sons of Israel of Bensonhurst

Founded in 1895 for summer residents, this cater-corner Orthodox sanctuary is now home to Russian immigrants. It was erected in 1919 by Emery Roth, who designed the Classical Revival synagogue with the Shield of David topping its copper dome and entrance doors filled with golden symbols relevant to Judaism. Look for the shofar and the Decalogue. A large white menorah sits above the entry's pediment and lights up the night.

2115 Benson (and 21st Avenue), Brooklyn, NY 11214; 718-372-4830

Sons of Israel entrance doors.

MUSLIM AMERICAN SOCIETY

Incorporated in 1993, this society reports that it is a religious, charitable, social, cultural and educational organization. Membership is opened to all Sunni Moslems committed to its vision, a virtuous and just American society, and committed to conveying Islam with "utmost clarity" to New York communities. Arabic is spoken in all services and English during social events. Families from Syria, Egypt, Pakistan and Palestine, along with Uzbekistan, worship in this former catering hall that was opened in 2002 and refitted with a prayer room and a youth center for athletic programs. While the lobby still has crystal chandeliers and some mirrored walls, its carpeted prayer room contains the imam's minbar and segregated areas for prayer.

The stucco exterior of the rectangular building has been resurfaced, while a modern glass and chrome canopy features the center's name. Across the street, a handsome red brick building from 1903 is home to the Sixty-second Precinct police station. Both corner buildings span the neighborhood's architectural history from the beginning to the end of the twentieth century.

1933 Bath Avenue (at 20th Street), Brooklyn, NY 11214; 718-232-5905

Gravesend

Founded by Lady Deborah Moody, Gravesend is recorded as the sixth town in Brooklyn. Lady Moody received a charter from the Dutch, who guaranteed religious freedom and self-government through town meetings. She immigrated to the area in 1645 with a group of Anabaptists, who had continued to suffer religious persecution in their New England settlement. Anabaptists were members of a sixteenth-century European Christian reform movement who believed in baptism for all believers and separation of church and state.

Until 1685, Gravesend, also an English city on the Thames River, was the seat of King's County before that designation was bestowed on Flatbush. During the American Revolution, the British camped here with a huge army of twenty thousand, with four hundred ships anchored in the bay. The town remained a farm and fishing community until the 1800s, when it became a fashionable holiday destination—hotels, racetracks, casinos and amusement parks would be part of its development. It united with Brooklyn in 1894 but once included all the neighborhoods by the sea. Today, Coney Island, Sheepshead Bay, Sea Gate, Manhattan and Brighton Beaches have forged their own identities.

Private homes started to be built in the 1920s by Italian and Jewish settlers from up north and continued to be added into the 1950s, when the New York City housing project Marlboro Houses was developed on 86th Street. Sacred havens number more than fifteen, including eight synagogues with Syrian Orthodox majorities.

Part II

Gravesend Cemetery

These 1.6 acres, thought to date back to 1650, are together the oldest cemetery in New York City. After centuries of neglect, it was restored in 1972 by the Gravesend Historical Society, but seventeenth-century headstones are illegible, and the resting place of Lady Deborah Moody cannot be located. Grave markers from the eighteenth and nineteenth centuries are still legible on the landmark site, and families interred include the Dyckmans, Wycoffs, Van Pelts and Van Sicklens, who have their own section. Since it is thought that Lady Moody's home site was at 27 Gravesend Neck Road, neighbors say that her spirit still walks among them. The cemetery is located on Gravesend Neck Road at McDonald Avenue.

Gravesend Cemetery.

First Korean Church of Brooklyn

The Coney Island Christian Church, founded in 1925 by an Italian group, erected this sanctuary by architect R.T. Schaeffer on the corner site in 1937. See the cornerstone inscribed in Italian and the name of the gray ashlar

SACRED HAVENS OF BROOKLYN

church engraved high on the side wall under the crenellated roofline. The present Korean Evangelical Christian congregation purchased the property after the Coney Island Christians relocated in 1979 (see Trinity Tabernacle entry), and it added its name in bronze letters under the original nameplate. Gothic windows hold clear glass, and the intimate interior focuses on a large cross resting on white satin drapery in the apse.

14 Gravesend Neck Road (and Van Sicklen Avenue), Brooklyn, NY 11223; 718-265-2584

MIDRASH MOSHE BEN MAIMON

Due to the growing need of Jewish Orthodox residents from Syria, Lebanon and Israel, this new synagogue was built in 2012. The modern white-brick façade with one huge window over single entrance doors is resting on a granite veranda encircled with a black railing that features Shields of David.

59 West 1ˢᵗ Avenue, Brooklyn, NY 11223

TRINITY TABERNACLE OF GRAVESEND

The Gravesend Dutch Reform Church, dating from 1655, built this Gothic Revival design by J.G. Glover in 1894. It was the fourth building for a congregation that had moved to this site to escape the noisy Coney Island railroad line. Peter Van Note is credited for the carpentry work and Berville Schweimler as the mason. The Coney Island Christian Church moved from its small church to this property in 1979 and changed its name since it was nowhere near Coney Island. The congregation was founded in 1925 by Italian Pentecostal immigrants led by Reverend Giuseppe Greco and his wife, Rose.

The red brick exterior with terra-cotta trim and multiple gables is surrounded by a generous garden and a wrought-iron fence. Since the interior sanctuary was completely remodeled, the only reminders of the founding congregation are brass chandeliers, carved wood stairwells and stained-glass windows of vividly colored abstract patterns throughout the building. The nave's windows hold small roundels of Christian symbols: sheaves of wheat representing the body of Christ, the wine cup for the blood of Christ and the

140

Trinity Tabernacle of Gravesend.

dove of peace. Dozens of national flags hang from the balcony, representing the present congregation, which has invigorated the historical sanctuary.

121 Gravesend Neck Road (corner of 1ˢᵗ Street), Brooklyn, NY 11223; 718-998-7827

STS. SIMON AND JUDE CHURCH

In 1897, Reverend William Gardiner was assigned to start the first Roman Catholic parish in Gravesend. He held services in a local store until a wooden church could be constructed the following year. Today's modern sanctuary, the Neo-Romanesque church built in 1966 on the original site, remembers two martyred disciples of Jesus. Its brick portal with five round arches leads to the tripartite entrance. Mosaic images of the patrons, along with the lamp of knowledge, are placed under the rose window. The interior's apse focuses on an enormous mosaic of the Crucifixion as a symbol of salvation.

185 Van Sicklen Street (Avenue T and Lake Avenue), Brooklyn, NY 11223; 718-375-9600

SHAARE ZION CONGREGATION

This sanctuary represents the largest Syrian Orthodox Sephardic congregation in North America, with minorities from Lebanon, Egypt, Morocco, Tunisia and Algeria. It was founded in 1950 by prosperous descendants of earlier Syrian immigrants and expanded rapidly as political problems escalated in the Middle East.

Today's modern round building was designed in 1958 by Morris Lapidus, well known for his theatrical Florida hotels. The façade's clear glass windows hold the symbol of the Magen David (Shield of David), while the interior is cantilevered to offer seating that separates men and women. Free-standing units for Torah scrolls (containing the five books of the Bible) are encased in precious metal, and services conducted from the center of the synagogue that can seat more than two thousand.

2030 Ocean Parkway (between Avenues T and U); 718-375-3834

BY THE WAY

On the exterior of the Sephardic Community Center, look for the wrought-iron sign with palm trees reflecting Middle Eastern origins of this meetinghouse, which sponsors cultural and recreational programs (1901 Ocean Parkway). The neighborhood's Orthodox congregations include Ahi Ezer Congregation (1885 Ocean Parkway and Avenue S), with a lavish wood-paneled interior and Torahs enclosed in a floor-to-ceiling column of stained glass. The modern corner building sits within an enclave of pricey private homes filled with emigrants who had left Syria in the 1990s. They settled in this tightly knit community that was formerly established in the early 1900s by Damascus and Aleppo Jews who came from the Lower East Side of Manhattan.

Other sanctuaries include Beach Haven Jewish Center at 723 Avenue Z (718-375-5200), Ahavath Achim at 1750 East 4th Street (718-375-3895), Sephardic Synagogue at 511 Avenue R (718-998-8171), Young Israel of Ocean Parkway at 1781 Ocean Parkway (718-376-6305) and Beth-El of Bensonhurst (House of God), opened by a Conservative congregation that borders the nearby neighborhood—hence its name.

1656 West 10th Street; 718-232-0019

Flatlands

As part of the oldest Dutch settlement established in 1636, the area was named Nieuw Amersfoort for the Dutch city in Utrecht. After the British took over in 1664, they renamed the area Flatlands for the land's typography. Original settlers maintained their Dutch roots and farmhouses, and some fine examples are still standing. The Pieter Claesen Wyckoff Home, built in 1641 and restored in 1982, is opened to the public at Clarendon Road and Ralph Avenue at East 59th Street (718-629-5400). Historical homes from the 1800s remain throughout the neighborhood.

Flatlands was absorbed into Brooklyn in 1896, but the area remained rural into the twentieth century. Its land once included Canarsie and East Flatbush, as well as Marine Park, developed in the late 1920s around an 798-acre park with a one-mile nature trail; Mill Basin, named after Dutch grain mills from 1664 and which would evolve into a residential area with docks and yacht clubs; and Bergen Beach, the popular summer community, which is presently filled with expensive custom-built homes.

Major development originated with the opening of the modern Kings Highway, which had been a passage of lanes and trails pieced together from the 1700s. Flatbush Avenue was completed in 1880 as an outgrowth of Prospect Park. The routes gave easy access to Irish, Italian and Jewish settlers migrating from Bedford-Stuyvesant and Bushwick in their new automobiles. More than twenty sacred havens have been built in Flatlands, with another fifteen in nearby Kings Highway.

FLATLANDS DUTCH REFORMED CHURCH

In about 1625, before the Dutch settled on Long Island, the Native American Canarsie tribe utilized this site for sacred rituals. After the Dutch purchased the Carnarsies' land, they built an octagonal church in 1663 by the orders of Peter Stuyvesant, who also ordered all colonists, regardless of their beliefs, to attend Dutch churches. Church archives report that designated family pews in this church were such a great asset that they were listed in property deeds.

The present landmark church, with its steeple still towering over the neighborhood, was built in 1848 by Henry Eldert; it was restored following fire damage in 1977. The Greek Revival design, with white clapboard siding and clear glass windows, remains surrounded by trees and green gardens. Be sure to visit the adjacent cemetery filled with Dutch settlers whose prominent names are seen on local street signs, including Wyckoff, Lott and Voorhees. Native Americans are also thought to be eternally resting in their original sacred grounds, making this spot ideal for restoring your spirit.

Kings Highway and East 40th Street, Brooklyn, NY 11226; 718-284-5140

BY THE WAY

The Mary Queen of Heaven Roman Catholic Church was founded in Old Mill Basin during 1927 by early Irish settlers. While the church's interior was destroyed by fire in 1997, a skillful restoration has assured that this haven will remain involved with the community. It is located at 1395 East 56th Street (and Avenue M) (718-763-2330).

As the Catholic population continued to grow, St. Bernard Roman Catholic Church was started in 1961 in an outdoor tent. In 1989, the modern brick church, with floor-length windows and a clear leaded-glass skylight, was dedicated near Bergen Beach. It is located at 2055 East 69th Street (718-763-5533)

St. Columba Roman Catholic Church is a modern, light brick sanctuary with a glorious figurative stained-glass wall, dedicated in 1967. It is located at 2245 Kimball St. (and Avenue U) (718-338-6265).

Eglise de Dieu de la Etoile du Matin is a French-speaking Caribbean Christian congregation that started to settle in the area in the 1980s and began their church at 1832 Schenectady Avenue.

FLATLANDS SYNAGOGUES

Temple Hillel of Flatlands is a Conservative congregation that was formed in the 1920s by residents who were on the move from north Brooklyn while various synagogues began to develop around affordable real estate found within the Flatlands area. With the influx of Middle Eastern immigrants in the 1990s, new Israeli members would greatly influence ritual, and in 2005, there was change in the temple's orientation to Orthodox methodology, with Hebrew widely spoken in the community. It is located at 2164 Ralph Avenue and Avenue L (718-763-2400).

The Madison Jewish Center is the only Egalitarian Conservative synagogue in the area. It was founded in 1931, with the congregation dedicating its second synagogue in 1949 and making a major addition to the building in 1951. It is located at 2989 Nostrand Avenue (718-375-2271).

Marine Park Jewish Center began in 1931 and is at 3311 Avenue S (718-375-0373).

Young Israel of Mill Basin, another Orthodox group, is located at 2082 East 58th Street (718-241-6982).

Flatbush Park Jewish Center, an Orthodox group founded in 1952, is at 6363 Avenue U (718-444-6868).

Meanwhile, the major transportation arteries of Kings Highway and Ocean Parkway created a huge shopping strip in the 1930s, along with many synagogues. The handsome Jewish Center of Kings Highway, a two-story Classical Revival building from 1928, was designed by Maurice Courland for the founding Conservative group. It has been listed on the National Register of Historic Places since 2010. The community is now home to large clusters of Russian Jewish immigrants. It is located at 1202 Avenue P (718-645-9000).

Borough Park

There is no park in this crowded neighborhood, once an original section of New Utrecht developed by Edwin Litchfield and called Blythebourne. In the 1880s, Irish immigrants arrived; in the early 1900s, Italians relocated from Manhattan, while Orthodox Jews migrated from Williamsburg. After World War II, Hasidim sects came in enormous numbers and now fill 80 percent of the neighborhood, residing along with Asian and Hispanic immigrants and a minority of original descendants. There are five churches, the first begun in 1891, nestled among dozens of synagogues whose histories date back to 1904 when Temple Emanu-El was founded by a long-departed Jewish Conservative community.

Multitudes of Russian, Israeli and European Jews arrived in the 1960s as former residents were relocating to suburbia. More than a dozen Brooklyn Hasidim sects reside here: Satmar, Chabad (or Lubavitch), Ger, Viznitz, Belz, Skve, Spinka, Pupa, Breslov, Rachmastrivk and Toldos Aharon.

The Bobover Hasidim, who first settled in Williamsburg, now dominate the community, whose members must live within walking distance to synagogues. The many stores stretching along 13th and 14th Avenues close for the Sabbath, which is observed from Friday afternoon to Saturday evening. Many synagogues are in private homes and unavailable to the general public.

FIRST CONGREGATION ANSHE SFARD

An Orthodox Sephardic congregation built this sanctuary in 1915 and placed its Hebrew name, *Anshe Sfard* ("People of Spain"), on the entrance gate. The red brick Classical Revival building, surrounded by its original black wrought-iron fence, has a portico with stone columns and tripartite entrance whose tympana are each filled with the stained-glass Shield of David. Interior wood panels feature carved images of musical instruments, while the bema (reader's platform) in the center of the sanctuary retains its lamps with antique globes. A huge marble-faced community center was built next door for social and cultural events and dwarfs the charming synagogue, reminding visitors of the community's growth.

In 1654, Sephardic Jews from Brazil arrived in New Netherlands and held services in secret since the Dutch government was intolerant of any form of worship other than in its sanctuary. With colonial America forming, Shearith Israel officially became the only Jewish congregation in New York

Congregation Anshe Sfard.

City until 1825. Between 1815 and 1825, immigration from central Europe would lead to the formation of Ashkenazi (German) synagogues.

4502 14th Avenue (between 45th and 46th Streets), Brooklyn, NY 11219; 718-436-2691

BY THE WAY

Young Israel Beth-El of Borough Park is a merged Orthodox congregation that was founded in 1906 as Temple Beth El and joined with Young Israel of Borough Park in 1988. The Romanesque brick sanctuary, designed by Shampan & Shampan in 1920, has an exterior archway with the Shield of David tympanum and an interior sanctuary with seating for two thousand worshipers. It is located at 4802 15th Avenue (at 48th Street), Brooklyn, New York, 11219 (718-435-9020). Shomrei Emunah was formed in 1908 by an Orthodox congregation, which built this yellow-brick Romanesque house of worship in 1910. An original skylight is still filled with charming floral patterns. It is located at 5202 14th Avenue, Brooklyn, New York, 11219 (718-851-8586). Temple Emanu-el, a Conservative congregation, built this Georgian red brick sanctuary in 1904, the first in the neighborhood. Because of demographic changes, it now belongs to the Satmar Hasidim, who adapted the synagogue and schoolbuilding for their rituals. It is located at 1364 49th Street (and 14th Avenue).

BOBOVER HASIDIM WORLD HEADQUARTERS

Poland had the greatest Hasidim concentration in eastern Europe before World War II. In almost every town, these sects were known for mystical practices and were centered on a revered leader, but they were said to have been at odds with traditional Orthodox communities.

Bobov, the largest Hasidim community in Borough Park, is named after the Polish town where founder Rebbe Rav Shlomo Halbershtam lived; his son and successor was killed during World War II. His grandson, Shlomo, immigrated to Crown Heights with a group of survivors who eventually came to Borough Hall. Shlomo died here in 2000 and was succeeded by his sons Naftuli and Bantziyon, now each having their own branch.

Hasidim once lived in villages known as "shtetls," with men dressing in eighteenth-century garments. Re-creating this lifestyle in Brooklyn, they reject the secular world and embrace the fundamentalist belief that scripture is the revealed word of God. Hebrew—spoken, written and read by all members—is also the language used on neighborhood signs. Nearly every block has a religious school or a house of worship. Boys and girls are traditionally segregated in yeshivas (schools), and the local library carries books in English, Hebrew and Yiddish. All restaurants offering Italian, Chinese and Middle Eastern foods are kosher. Joyous prayer is celebrated within synagogues, which have huge open spaces for men to sing and dance when they gather with the rebbe (spiritual leader). These spirited gatherings often spill out into the streets.

4909 15th Avenue (near 49th Street), Brooklyn, NY 11219; 718-853-7900

BOROUGH PARK PROGRESSIVE TEMPLE (CONGREGATION BETH AHAVATH SHOLOM)

Almost lost among Orthodox and Hasidic synagogues, this sole Reform temple reflects innovations attributed to freedom of worship in America. The group was founded in 1919, with its vision of "the right to interpret the teachings of Israel of the past in the light of the present." Equal rights were given to all men and women; families prayed and sat together at services, and rituals, reflecting the spirit of Reform Judaism, continued to preserve their tradition, which centered on the Torah.

The founding group purchased the Borough Park Presbyterian Church, originally on the 15th Street corner of the large land tract, and moved the

Borough Park Progressive Temple.

149

building down 46th Street to the back of the property, which is now its present location. By selling the front acreage, the members were in a better financial position than most new congregations. But they became a minute presence among the influx of Hasidim immigrants in the 1950s and would survive the overwhelming odds by merging with Beth Ahavath Sholom in 2005 to continue their spirited celebrations and mitzvah (good works) projects.

The white aluminum-sided temple features its name prominently on the façade, which also has a historic remnant of stained glass in a half-moon window. With its pitched roof crowned by the Shield of David's brass icon, the temple has continued in the spirit of the founders and remains a shining light tucked among private residences.

1515 46th Street (and 15th Avenue), Brooklyn, NY 11219; 718-436-5082

ST. FRANCIS DE CHANTAL ROMAN CATHOLIC CHURCH

The congregation was founded in 1891 in Maggie Gorman's home on 56th Street, where the first Mass was celebrated, with 125 in attendance. After the present site was purchased, a small frame church was built for the Irish

Stained-glass anchor in St. Francis de Chantal Church.

congregation, and by 1925, the present church had been dedicated, with enough oak pews to seat 1,000.

The Neo-Romanesque corner building, with a wheel window highlighting its light brick façade, is enhanced by a generous garden holding the Crucifixion shrine and an enormous bronze image of Pope John Paul II. Services held in English, Spanish and Polish reflect the diversity of today's community.

A round chancel filled with white marble and a pair of angels kneeling in adoration in the apse enhance the barrel-vaulted interior. Stained-glass windows line the side aisles, while two more angels offer holy water at the entrance doors. Old art glass fills the tympana, and an anchor's image acts as a reminder of earlier parishioners who labored in the Brooklyn Navy Yard.

Patron Francis de Chantal (1572–1641), who was born in Dijon, France, was a noblewoman, a wife, a mother of four, a widow at age twenty-eight and, along with her mentor Francis de Sales, a founder of the Visitation Sisters. See her portrait in the chapel and another full-length image in the nave's side aisle. Also note the large portrait of Our Lady of Czestochowa, an icon that recognizes Polish members in the congregation.

1273 58th Street (and 12th Avenue), Brooklyn, NY 11219; 718-436-6407

CHRIST EVANGELICAL LUTHERAN CHURCH

Scandinavian immigrants founded this congregation in 1899. As the population grew, they built the present light brick church in 1930, right next door to the old sanctuary, which was demolished, and its space was utilized as a yard for community celebrations. The pastor's white clapboard house still stands on the property, while a banner, printed with the sanctuary's name in English and Mandarin Chinese, is evidence that the congregation has welcomed yet another immigrant group.

A serene interior, with an open timbered-ceiling, is lined with stained-glass windows enhanced with small roundels and unique limestone tracery. Look for the stylized lamp signifying spiritual light and the Torah scroll for biblical teachings.

1066 59th Street, Brooklyn, NY 11219; 718-972-2517

ST. CATHERINE OF ALEXANDRIA ROMAN CATHOLIC CHURCH

This Romanesque church is located on the Borough Park border in Kensington, a small neighborhood with Green-Wood Cemetery to its north. Founded in 1902, the congregation first held services in a loft on 39th Street, until it was financially stable enough to build a church. Its patron, Catherine, an aristocrat, embraced Christianity in the fourth century while defying Emperor Maxentius, who tried to have her executed on a machine of wheels and blades. She is often portrayed holding the torturous instrument, popularly known as the Catherine Wheel; the wheel broke, and she was then beheaded.

The sanctuary's majestic exterior holds a round limestone wheel window filled with tracery that is reminiscent of the Catherine Wheel and also has the tallest copper steeple in the neighborhood. Veterans are remembered at an outdoor shrine of *The Pieta* (the dead Jesus lying across the knees of his mother),while an outdoor grotto of Our Lady of Lourdes recalls the apparitions of Mary to Bernadette, a humble peasant girl in Lourdes, France. The barrel-vaulted interior, seating more than seven hundred, is filled with decorative furnishings and tall lancet windows holding small roundels that tell the life story of Jesus. Look for golden mosaic images in the apse, including St. Catherine.

1119 41st Street (and Fort Hamilton Parkway), Brooklyn, NY 11218; 718-436-5917

Flatbush

East Flatbush, Midwood, Prospect Park South and Ditmas Park

Centrally located, Flatbush was the heart of Brooklyn, but it is now divided into four postal codes and miniature neighborhoods. Its Dutch name, *Vlackebos*, tells of a wood-filled landscape, but after a railroad opened in 1878, farmland began evolving into fashionable residential communities. In 1920, the Brighton Beach subway line brought the development of large apartment houses along Ocean Avenue and down to Kings Highway. Ebbets Field, home of the Brooklyn Dodgers from 1915 until 1957, also made the neighborhood a well-known location. Following World War II, Middle Easterners, Koreans and Russians moved into the area. In the 1980s, Caribbean immigrants, with a majority from Haiti, added more diversity to this former Dutch settlement from 1652. The land had once belonged to the Canarsie Indians and remained rural farmland for more than two hundred years. From 1658 until 1832, Flatbush held the Main Courthouse for Kings County until it was destroyed by fire. After 1825, when streets were planned, Flatbush Avenue became the main artery that would extend from downtown Brooklyn to the Flatlands.

In 1873, Flatbush citizens fought to remain independent and refused to become part of the city of Brooklyn. To hold public meetings, Flatbush Town Hall was built in 1875 and still stands at 35 Snyder Avenue; the red brick Victorian Gothic landmark is now a public school. Alas, in 1894, Flatbush was annexed by Brooklyn right before the big merger in 1898 with New York City.

Ocean Parkway, itself a landmark, runs six scenic miles and connects Prospect Park to Coney Island. Its original northern section was destroyed for the later Prospect Expressway. Since housing is needed within walking distance to synagogues, many pricey homes and yeshivas (religious schools) have been built by Sephardic Syrians from Aleppo and Damascus. Ashkenazi Jews from Europe were the first to settle here in the 1920s and still have their German bakeries and grocery stores.

The newer Flatbush borders contain more than ninety-two sacred havens, including thirteen French-speaking churches and fifteen synagogues. East Flatbush has sixty-three churches and five synagogues. Vander Veer, the neighborhood around Brooklyn College, has thirty-three churches and four synagogues. The borders of Flatbush are continually shifting as real estate developers continue to rename land tracts to appeal to a trendier segment of the population.

FLATBUSH REFORMED DUTCH CHURCH

The oldest New York City congregation from 1655 is now located in the heart of busy Flatbush. It is the most famous sacred haven in Brooklyn, with a graveyard testifying to its Dutch history. Erasmus High School evolved from the

church's first private school in 1786 and became part of the public school system in 1886. Look for the bronze sculptured image of the sixteenth-century Dutch scholar Desiderius Erasmus, standing with an air of authority in front of the original academy from 1786. The landmark wooden building is scheduled to become the Caribbean American Chamber of Commerce and Industry, perhaps saluting one of the academy's founders, Alexander Hamilton (circa 1755–1804), who was born in the British West Indies.

The church's original site now holds its third building, constructed from 1793 to 1798 by Thomas Fardon. It is a Federal-style landmark built of local

Flatbush Reformed Church, now in the center of the business district.

stone, wood and brick and is set on its predecessor's 1699 foundation. The main entrance is beneath a square clock tower that holds an octagonal wooden lantern, sculptured urns and a handsome spire with a unique weathervane. Its cemetery holds early Dutch families, including Vanderbilts, Lotts, Leffertses, Cortelyous, Bergens and Ditmases—all familiar names of streets and avenues. Be sure to see early twentieth-century homes in the small Albemarle-Kenmore Terraces Historic District, located behind the church property.

890 Flatbush Avenue (corner of Church Avenue), Brooklyn, NY 11226; 718-284-5140

St. Paul's Episcopal Church

Founded in 1836 as a chapel for British descendants of colonial settlers, the church has been revitalized by Caribbean immigrants from former British colonies where the Anglican Church remained prominent. The large Gothic Revival sanctuary (built in 1877) easily holds its 1,500 members and displays both church and national flags that represent the community. Sanctuary

St. Paul's Episcopal Church.

windows donated by Anglican families are filled with biblical scenes and a portrait of the founding chapel. The congregation now celebrates with some of its own traditions, such as the Harvest Mass, giving thanks with offerings of corn stalks and including steel drums and guitars along with traditional organ music.

157 St. Paul's Place (19th Street between Church and Caton Avenue), Brooklyn, NY; 718-282-2100

BY THE WAY

This Caribbean community also worships at twelve other French-language churches in the neigborhood. Along Nostrand Avenue, look for Eglise de Dieu de la Fraternalle at 1709, Eglise La Verite at 1024 and Bethanie French Seventh-Day Adventist at 2059 Bedford Avenue, holding services on Saturday.

St. Mark's United Methodist Church (at 2017 Beverly Road and Ocean Avenue, 718-282-6304) was organized in 1903 by migrants from downtown Brooklyn and has sponsored three other congregations, which worship in its sanctuary: Premiere Eglise Methodiste Unie (First United Methodist), Kings Highway United Methodist and Ghana Wesley United Methodist. Methodist Hospital was also the earlier congregation's project.

FLATBUSH-TOMPKINS CONGREGATIONAL CHRISTIAN CHURCH

This Neo-Georgian design from 1910 by Allen and Collens, along with local architect Louis Jallade, is located in the historic district of Ditmas Park. This area was developed in 1902 by Louis Pounds, who not only divided the area for country homes but also planted the present trees. Its streets are lined with Victorian homes that open for an annual tour. This sacred haven is the most prominent building in the residential neighborhood filled with architectural gems.

424 East 19th Street (between Ditmas Avenue and Dorchester Road), Brooklyn, NY 11226; 718-282-5353

MASJID (MOSQUE) ABOU BAKR EL SEDDIQUE

This red brick mosque in a renovated home was founded by Pakistani Moslem settlers who had opened local businesses. It is notorious for the presence of the Blind Sheikh, Omar Rahman, who arrived in the United States in 1990 and preached in three local mosques, encouraging radical followers to acts of terrorism. Rahman is now serving a life sentence for terrorist activities. Islam is based on the teachings of the Prophet Muhammad, whose life was filled with many revelations, all of which are collected in the Quran.

115 Foster Avenue (McDonald Avenue and 47th Street), Brooklyn, NY 11230; 718-871-8815

OUR LADY OF REFUGE

This Flatbush neighborhood around Brooklyn College is known as Vander Veer, and the local post office is still identified by the Dutch family name. A Roman Catholic Irish group begun to meet on this site in 1911 and first built a one-story brick church the following year. In 1934, the members moved into the present granite church, designed by Brooklyn architect Henry V. Murphy in his own French Gothic style. This exterior façade holds a huge rectangular window with stone tracery forming a Celtic cross to reflect the Irish roots, while the interior walls, piers and arches are red brick. Fifteen stained-glass windows portraying mysteries of the rosary (events in the life of Jesus and his mother Mary) line the sanctuary, which is 186 feet long and 55 feet wide. Look up to the balcony for an interesting wrought-iron clock whose hours are represented by icons of the twelve apostles.

2020 Foster Avenue, Brooklyn, NY 11210, 718-434-2090

BY THE WAY

Testifying to the growth of Roman Catholics in Flatbush, two other churches were built after Our Lady of Refuge was well established. In 1923, St. Vincent Ferrer opened at 1603 Brooklyn Avenue (718-959-9029), and Our Lady Help of Christians opened in 1927 at 1315 East 28th Street (718-338-5242).

FLATBUSH SYNAGOGUES

Temple Beth Emeth v'Ohr Progressive Shaari Zedek is a Reform synagogue that three other congregations joined in the 1960s when neighborhood demographics started to shift. Today's building was dedicated in 1914 and was renovated in 1936 to include a handsome Art Deco bronze ark. Along with oak pews, wood wainscoting and colorful stained glass, the sanctuary is indeed a "little jewel box." The congregation practices Judaism "as a living fountain not frozen in time." It is located at 83 Marlborough Road and Church Avenue (718-282-1596).

Congregation B'nai Jacob of Flatbush is another Reform congregation, located at 3017 Glenwood Road (718-434-8855).

Young Israel of Vander Veer Park, an Orthodox synagogue for members living around Brooklyn College, is located at 2811 Farragut Road (718-434-2910).

Beth El Jewish Center of Flatbush, another Orthodox synagogue, built in 1927, is now in Homecrest, but note that Flatbush is still part of its name. It is located at 1981 Homecrest Avenue (at Avenue T).

East Midwood Jewish Center was built by a Conservative congregation that completed the huge Renaissance Revival structure with a small chapel and a two-story synagogue in 1929, just in time before Great Depression hit. The majestic center has been carefully preserved and is listed on the National Register of Historic Places. It is located at 1625 Ocean Avenue (between Avenues K and L).

ST. AUGUSTINE EPISCOPAL CHURCH

The former agricultural community of Dutch Flatbush held a huge population of slaves who settled in the area after slavery was abolished in New York in 1827. By the late nineteenth century, former farmhands were working-class citizens establishing homes and building sacred havens. This church in East Flatbush was founded in 1875 by an African American congregation that made history by evolving from the social activism of the 1920s to the civil rights movement in the 1950s. In 1969, when its church and school were destroyed by fire, the congregation began a nomadic existence until the members could purchase this building in 1982. They installed three stained-glass windows over the altar and added colorful murals to their serene interior. In 2003, the church was returned to its original full parish status and continues to sponsor youth programs, family ministries and senior citizen classes.

4311 Avenue D (and Troy Avenue), Brooklyn, NY; 718-629-0930

BY THE WAY

Other East Flatbush havens include Greater St. James AME Zion Church at 1158 Lenox Road (718-495-9702). Premier Baptist Church at 1014 Utica Avenue (718-346-8903) is one of many Baptist churches in the community. St. Therese of Liseux Roman Catholic Church was founded in 1926 by Brooklyn migrants who were seeking greener pastures at 1281 Troy Avenue (and Avenue D), Brooklyn, New York, 11203 (718-451-1500).

HOLY INNOCENTS

Monsignor John T. Woods, pastor of Holy Cross Roman Catholic Church, founded in 1845, witnessed enormous growth in the area and petitioned Bishop Charles McDonnell to start this parish. A private frame house was utilized in 1909, with 25 in the congregation, and within the year, a temporary church seating 400 had been built on the present site. Additional property was acquired to build today's English Gothic sanctuary, designed by Helmle & Corbett and dedicated in 1923. Records show the devastating effect of the 1929 financial crash on the new church, but by 1938, the congregation had 5,700 members. Interior stone walls are enhanced by stained-glass windows by John Morgan & Son, while the furnishings were designed by the architects. Mural paintings by artist Tabor Sears add great beauty to the nave, especially the huge painting of the Holy Innocents that dominates the apse, showing the children of Bethlehem who were massacred by King Herod surrounding the heavenly throne.

279 East 17th Street (and Beverly Road), Brooklyn, NY 11226, 718-469-9500

CHURCH AVENUE

Along with heavy traffic and MTA bus service, Church Avenue is home to hundreds of businesses, grocery stores and bakeries for Caribbean, Latino,

The Flatbush Fire Department bell from 1893 at Church of the Holy Redeemer.

Indian and Pakistani settlers, as well as more than fifteen churches, hence its name.

Church of the Holy Redeemer was once a firehouse, and the Christian congregation has the Flatbush Fire Department's large bell from 1893 in the front yard at number 2267 (718-693-9386). New Jerusalem Church of the Nazarene includes French signage for Caribbean members at number 2431 (718-287-0891). Holy Cross Roman Catholic Church, founded in 1845 at number 2530, occupies a huge site with a school and a separate red brick chapel adorned with colorful tiles at the far end of the avenue (718-469-5900). Eglise de Dieu, at number 3921, holds services for French-speaking Caribbeans. Pentecostal Gospel Tabernacle at number 5407 (718-498-1998) is part of the Pentecostal movement that began in the American South in about 1900 and has a diverse congregation, which participates in the service's gospel music. Brooklyn Faith Seventh-Day Adventist at number 5518 (718-282-1317) celebrates its Sabbath on Saturday.

Part III

Carlmelo Booc.

Bedford-Stuyvesant

Bedford was founded by Lord Bedford, a Dutchman, in the 1660s and organized by English governor Richard Nicolls in 1677, while Stuyvesant Heights, named for the sixth and last Dutch governor, Peter Stuyvesant, was part of Bedford's farmland and became a Dutch town in 1663. They would both be designated as wards of the newly incorporated city of Brooklyn in 1834. When the State of New York abolished slavery in 1827, freed slaves who had labored on local farms developed self-reliant communities in nearby Weeksville and Carrsville.

The Brooklyn and Jamaica Railroad (now the Long Island Railroad) brought middle-class white residents to homes built on speculation in the 1880s. Here they joined prosperous businessmen already residing in large mansions, including Frank Woolworth of the Woolworth five-and-dime stores, now Foot Locker, and Abraham Abraham, founder of Abraham & Straus Department Store, now Macy's. Many sacred havens were built as part of the development to appeal to upwardly mobile prospective tenants.

After World War II, the area with a black population of about 4 percent felt the beginning of middle-class relocation to suburbia. In 1936, the A subway line opened a new commuting corridor from Brooklyn to Manhattan's Harlem, while downtown black churches began moving into the neighborhood, causing racial tension to heighten among the predominantly white population.

During World War II, many residents worked at the Brooklyn Navy Yard, and the black population grew to 25 percent, but after the war, returning veterans led the flight to suburbia. By 1970, Bed-Stuy had become the city's largest black community, surpassing Harlem, and many residents would make major contributions to city life. Arturo Schomburg became a private collector of black history when he was told that no history existed; Harlem's leading research center and public library is named in his honor. Shirley Chisholm served as a United States congresswoman for six terms and ran for U.S. president. Lena Horne, singer and film star; Jackie Robinson, the first black baseball player for the Brooklyn Dodgers; Earl Graves, publisher of *Black Enterprise* magazine; and film director Spike Lee were all products of the community.

But among the many unsung heroes are hundreds of pastors who, like their predecessors, continued to care for the neighborhood's spiritual and temporal needs. Many early pastors were abolitionists and established underground passages for runaway slaves on their way to Canada. When you visit their sanctuaries, you'll see that every day is a celebration of black history, with displayed photos of noble pastors, Tuskegee airmen and other neighborhood heroes who made a difference. Brooklyn-born Sarah Keys Evans was a member of the U.S. Army Women's Corps in 1952 and was in full uniform when she was told to give up her seat on an interstate bus that had passed into Alabama. Sarah said no and became one of the reasons that the Interstate Commerce Commission passed legislation forbidding race-based rules on any interstate bus. The national civil rights movement was dawning, and under the leadership of local church pastors, congregations marched united for social justice in the 1960s. Within Bedford-Stuyvesant, there are more than two hundred sacred havens, with services conducted in English, Spanish and French and meetings held in traditional church buildings, converted residences and storefront chapels.

Antioch Baptist Church

Founded in 1854 as the Greene Avenue Baptist Church, this landmark sanctuary was said to have been financially assisted by the Rockefeller family, who helped many Baptist groups. The church was antifundamentalist in its beliefs but always opened to new ideas. Records show that in 1922 the congregation played host to William Jennings Bryan to hear his speech against Darwinism.

In 1950, the remaining white congregation sold the property to the downtown Antioch Baptists, who were founded in 1918 by Reverend Moses P.

Paylor. Before Paylor died in 1958, he saw his church become one of the borough's most prominent African American congregations. His successor, Reverend George Lawrence, served the congregation until his death in 1983; as an associate of Reverend Martin Luther King Jr., Lawrence led the congregation through civil rights struggles and neighborhood revival programs.

Look for the lower church's photo montage of celebrities and prominent preachers: the official spark of the civil rights movement, Rosa Parks; poet Langston Hughes, the voice of the Harlem Renaissance whose ashes are interred in the Arturo Schomberg Public Library; and the visit of Dr. King to the sanctuary.

Biblical lesson in stained glass at Antioch Baptist Church.

Built from 1887 to 1892, the church was designed in the Queen Anne style with Romanesque elements by Lansing C. Holden, with additions by Paul F. Higgs. The symmetrical façade has rock-faced brick in contrasting colors, with cast-iron and terra-cotta panels. Queen Anne architecture originated in England and along with the William Morris arts and crafts movement was popular in America in the late 1870s.

The exterior is divided into five components. The central bowed-bay section holds three stained-glass windows. It is flanked by two identical recessed units with brick towers, and end pavilions have long stone stairways with original railings and distinct roofs, one pyramid-shaped and the other a tall steeple, thus creating an interesting skyline.

The lower church, built by F. Mapes, was the first section to open in 1888. It holds five small windows installed by the original congregation and can seat almost six hundred. Due to financial restraints, the upper church took five years to complete.

Records from 1904 show huge crowds at services that made it necessary to add the gallery to the sanctuary. Stained-glass windows began to be installed in 1901, in memory of the original rector, Reverend Robert B. Montgomery. Opaque art glass works hold roundels with images of Jesus, but two figurative windows in the front of the sanctuary tell biblical tales. See young Jesus preaching to richly garbed rabbis, not unlike the congregation that continues to serve the community by good example and good deeds.

828 Greene Avenue (between Stuyvesant and Lewis Avenues), Brooklyn, NY 11221; 718-455-7778

HERBERT VON KING CULTURAL ARTS CENTER AND TOMPKINS PARK

Noted as the spot where young Beverly Sills (1929–2007) of the New York City Opera Company gave her first public performance, the New York City park designed in 1871 by Olmsted and Vaux remains a pleasant spot to rest. It was renamed by Mayor Edward Koch for local activist Herbert Von King (1912–1985). Former honoree Daniel Tompkins was governor of New York State and James Madison's vice president; he is also remembered in Manhattan's East Village Tompkins Square Park.

670 Lafayette Avenue (between Marcy and Tompkins Avenues), Brooklyn, NY 11216; 718-622-2082

VARICK MEMORIAL AME ZION CHURCH

Established in 1818 as Williamsburg's first black congregation, the church would relocate several times to sites in Weeksville and Fort Greene and change its name each time to its street designation. In the early 1900s, the congregation settled on Ralph Avenue before moving to the present site in 1950, where the sanctuary became known as the Church of Black Liberation as it participated in the 1960s civil rights struggle.

The congregation is named for James Varick, who with a handful of black members broke away from the white John Street Methodist Church in 1796 to form the African Chapel. The members later added Zion to their name to recall the biblical designation of a sacred site. These reformers established their first church on Leonard Street in downtown

Manhattan and elected Varick as the first bishop in 1822. He decreed that there was to be no distinction as to race, color or economic condition in the new chapel, and he became an organizer of the African Methodist Episcopal Zion Conference of Churches, which spread throughout the United States and Canada. Today, Bishop Varick is permanently resting in Mother AME Zion Church on West 137th Street in Manhattan, while his message of social justice remains an inspiration for all congregations.

806 Quincey Street (and Patchen Avenue), Brooklyn, NY 11221; 347-405-5306

ST. GEORGE'S EPISCOPAL CHURCH

This High Victorian Gothic church was designed in 1887 by Richard Michell Upjohn, son of noted architect Richard Upjohn, and was built as the third church for a white congregation organized in 1869 by Reverend Alvah Guion. Established as St. Thomas Episcopal Church, the congregation would have a name change to the Guion Church, honoring the founder. Finally, when becoming members of the Diocese of Long Island in 1869, the members would invoke the patronage of St. George. Fire in 1900 damaged the sanctuary, but rebuilding in 1906 left the red brick and brownstone landmark revitalized, having a garden on its corner lot. The charming exterior has a unique, squat octagonal tower, as well as a small entrance porch with miniature columns.

The warmth reflected in the cruciform interior is enhanced by dark walnut arches bordered by clerestory windows and original wood pews seating more than five hundred. Tiffany windows above the white marble reredos feature a rare Crucifixion scene in pale opalescent tones, along with the *Resurrection* window, which glows with a white-robed angel at the opened tomb. Two other Tiffany biblical scenes in the nave highlight the Samarian woman and Jesus accompanied by a child, with Jerusalem in the background. See an imposing Moses in a newer window donated by parishioners, who continue to replace original tinted-glass with relevant icons.

800 Marcy Avenue (between Monroe Street and Gates Avenue), Brooklyn, NY 11216; 718-789-6036

PART III

CONCORD BAPTIST CHURCH OF CHRIST

In 1848, Brooklyn members of Manhattan's Abyssinian Baptist Church, who traveled every Sunday by ferry across the East River, purchased a downtown site on Concord Street for Brooklyn's first black Baptist church and enlisted Reverend Sampson White, a former Abyssinian pastor, as their leader. Following a common practice, the new church was named for its street location, and like many downtown havens in the 1940s, Concord relocated but kept its former name after purchasing Marcy Baptist Church on the present site. That building was destroyed by fire in 1952 but was resurrected in 1956 as today's modern Romanesque sanctuary.

The main entrance is defined by a recessed arched portal with a dramatic wheel window above the tripartite entrance. Three limestone arches, enhanced by red wooden doors, carry engraved lintels with biblical messages: "Come Unto Me Ye Who Labor," "I Will Give You Rest" and "Take My Yoke Upon You." When entering the narthex, look for a small brass plaque that thanks Joseph Leito for donating his savings to rebuild the light brick church.

Red entrance doors of Concord Baptist Church.

Clear glass partitions in the narthex separate the serene modern nave, which is encircled by a wood-faced balcony able to seat 1,000; on the main floor, there is space for more than 2,300. The sanctuary's focus, a huge wooden cross, is enhanced by vertical drapery that conceals the baptismal pool. Well known for its music, this Christian congregation is probably one of the largest in New York City and has wisely included a soundproof children's room on the balcony.

Led through turbulent times by Reverend Gardner C. Taylor (1948–1990), the church opened an elementary school in 1960 and a nursing home in 1975. The dedicated pastor is honored with his name featured on the Marcy Avenue street sign.

833 Marcy Avenue (at Madison and Putnam Avenues), Brooklyn, NY 11216; 718-622-1818

SILOAM PRESBYTERIAN CHURCH

Reverend James Gloucester—whose father, a minister and former slave, had established the Presbyterian movement in Philadelphia for black congregations—opened a sanctuary in 1848 on downtown Fulton and Cranberry Streets. After several relocations, the present site was purchased in 1944 from the white congregation of Central Presbyterian Church, which had merged with the Bedford Avenue group. One part of the church was rebuilt in 1936 after a fire, but the congregation continues to utilize the section from the 1800s. Church archives report that abolitionist John Brown stopped here on his way to the U.S. Arsenal, Harper's Ferry, for the armed slave revolt in 1859, and he was given a twenty-five-dollar donation.

A serene cream-colored sanctuary remains unadorned but filled with natural light from translucent Palladian windows. *The Burning Bush*, a dark wooden sculpture, enhances the raised apse, which is filled with choir stalls and a black marble altar. In 1964, the church was headquarters for the public school boycott to improve education, led by its pastor, Reverend Milton A. Galamison, and the influential social activist Bayard Rustin (1912–1987). The congregation continued to demonstrate for equality and human dignity with its neighboring churches and remains a beacon of light for the community. Look for portraits of Reverend John Gloucester (1776–1822) and his son, James, in the narthex of the red brick Colonial-styled building.

260 Jefferson Avenue (between Marcy and Nostrand Avenues), Brooklyn, NY 11216; 718-789-7050

BRIDGE STREET AFRICAN WESLEYAN METHODIST EPISCOPAL CHURCH

Because so many members had moved to Bed-Stuy, Brooklyn's oldest black church purchased this site in 1938; it was built as Grace Presbyterian Church in 1891. The golden-brick Neo-Gothic exterior has a squat crenellated tower dominating its corner lot, while a narrow interior with a wood-vaulted ceiling seats more than seven hundred. Two huge stained-glass windows dominate the balcony with a charming image of Jesus among children.

The congregation was incorporated in 1818 by black members tired of segregated services in downtown Sands Street Methodist Episcopal Church, which was founded in 1766. Black members had been gathering for prayer since 1788 (the date noted on the church's cornerstone), and after first worshiping in private homes, the group built a small church in 1819. It also opened the first free school for black children and continued to prosper. In 1854, several mergers resulted in relocating to Bridge Street, a sanctuary built in 1846 as the First Free Congregational Church (now a landmark belonging to Pratt University). The congregation retained its last name for its future location.

Always socially active, the group supported the Underground Railroad and assured runaway slaves safe passage to freedom. In 1863, the sanctuary also assisted black refugees from Manhattan's Draft Riots, begun by white immigrants who opposed joining the armed forces but who were unable to make the necessary payments to escape serving in the Civil War.

Dr. Susan Smith-McKinney-Steward (1847–1918)—the first New York State black woman to become a medical doctor and only the third female physician in America—was Bridge Street's church organist and musical director. She belonged to an elite group, the Brooklyn Colored 400, which was fashioned after The 400, Manhattan socialites led by Mrs. Caroline Astor and her son, John. In 1885, some Bridge Street members left to establish the Fleet Street Church (see entry).

277 Stuyvesant Avenue (between Jefferson and Hancock Streets), Brooklyn, NY 11221; 718-452-3936

OUR LADY OF VICTORY ROMAN CATHOLIC CHURCH

In church records, it is stated that "these were turbulent times." The Civil War had ended, President Abraham Lincoln had been assassinated and his successor, Andrew Johnson, was almost impeached. In 1868, Reverend Patrick Creighton opened a sacred haven that would "foster dignity of man under God and to help fulfill the American dream that brought these people to America."

The congregation of Irish immigrants outgrew its smaller haven and with continuing prosperity dedicated the present Neo-Gothic church, designed by Thomas F. Houghton, in 1895. Parish records continued to reflect what was happening in American society and described economic depressions along with sacrifices during the war years. Major demographic shifts after World War II—when soldiers returned, married and moved to suburbia— saw the founding congregation replaced with African American and other ethnic families to carry on the church's mission.

The exterior of the dark, weathered-stone church has multiple towers and spires, while surrounding gates and woodwork painted bright red offer an attractive accent. The polychrome statue of brown-skinned Mary as Our Lady of Victory stands in a corner garden, while an additional image of the patron is sculptured in the tympanum over the main entrance.

Our Lady of Victory Garden.

An interior sanctuary that seats more than 1,200 is filled with Gothic arches and columns, a sky blue vaulted ceiling and huge stained-glass windows in the transept. Look in both windows for images of former pastors Woods and McCabe. An enormous wooden cross hanging above the chancel leads the way into the apse with its decorative marble reredos guarded by archangels and display of the black marble bust of Mary that was cast from Michelangelo's *Pieta*. Look up to the massive organ pipes in the gallery and imagine the sound once enjoyed during crowded recitals and concerts that brought fame to the church.

Today, the Missionaries of Charity, founded by Mother Teresa of Calcutta, tend to all service ministries and reside around the corner from the sanctuary. Meanwhile, Holy Rosary Church was administratively merged with Our Lady of Victory. Holy Rosary was begun in 1899 in a blacksmith shop; soon Hubbard's Peach and Apple Orchard was purchased to build its Neo-Romanesque sanctuary at 139 Chaucey Street (between Stuyvesant and Malcolm X Boulevard).

583 Throop Avenue (between Macon and McDonough Streets), Brooklyn, NY 11216; 718-919-2265

First AME Zion Church (Fleet Street Church)

In 1885, fifteen members of the Bridge Street Church (see entry) broke away to establish the downtown AME Zion sanctuary, informally known as the Fleet Street Church to identify its location. When the congregation shifted in the 1940s to Bed-Stuy, members purchased Tompkins Avenue Congregational Church, built in 1889 by George Chappell and able to hold more than two thousand worshipers.

The red brick Romanesque Revival design, with white woodwork trim, dominates its corner site with an impressive clock tower rising more than 140 feet. An auditorium-styled interior with round-headed pews and a wood-faced balcony is serenely lit by grass-green and marigold-yellow stained-glass windows. Golden organ pipes fill the apse above the wood reredos, with a focus on the white-lighted crucifix. The congregation has skillfully preserved its sanctuary and continues to play a role in neighborhood activities.

55 MacDonough Street (between Tompkins and Marcy Avenues); 718-638-3343

STUYVESANT HEIGHTS CHRISTIAN CHURCH, DISCIPLES OF CHRIST

Directly across the street from First AME Zion Church, this congregation resides in a red brick and limestone Gothic Revival building from 1873, built as Tompkins Avenue Presbyterian Church. It has huge arched windows and a front porch supported on slim columns that are graced by Corinthian capitals. The sanctuary also served as St. Matthew's Episcopal Church from 1889 to 1944, until the present congregation purchased the site. The black congregation was organized in 1928 as Calvary Christian Church in Manhattan, with Reverend William Montague Johnston, who would relocate the group that same year to downtown Brooklyn.

Painted brown wood rafters and buttresses outline the peaked interior roof in an opened cream-colored nave. Arched windows sparkle with original stained glass, some holding quatrefoil symbols (four-leaf design), which represent the New Testament's four evangelists. Sadly, one set of windows over the narrow wood-faced balcony has been lost, but both exterior and interior restoration

Stuyvesant Heights Christian Church.

of the sanctuary was undertaken in 2004. The church has been acclaimed for its Early Childhood Learning Center and summer camp.

69 MacDonough Street (between Tompkins and Marcy Avenues), Brooklyn, NY 11216; 718-783-5383

ST. PHILIP'S EPISCOPAL CHURCH

During 1944, the Church of the Good Shepherd's white congregation was dwindling, which caused the Episcopal Diocese to invite St. Philip's black members from nearby Weeksville to utilize this historic sanctuary. The group, founded in 1900 at 1610 Dean Street, dedicated its new home to the apostle who converted Ethiopians to Christianity. The sanctuary, extending through the middle of a city block, connects to the large Decatur Avenue red brick conference center erected in 1905.

The English Gothic Revival stone church, with ornamented entry porch, was designed by Arne Delhi in 1899 with no expense spared. The interior, seating more than five hundred, holds glorious artifacts from both founding and present members. Fourteen Stations of the Cross are fashioned in solid-colored textiles, making this modern artwork a perfect contrast among Gothic arches and elaborately carved ornaments. Above the white marble altar with a gilded trimmed reredos, an enormous stained-glass window recalls the sanctuary's original designation, the Good Shepherd, with Jesus in the hills of Jerusalem, accompanied by children and sheep. It is one of four windows in the church signed by Charles Maggin. Be sure to see the window of young Jesus preaching to the elders in the temple, an elaborate design resembling a medieval triptych. Four white-robed angels hold a banner declaring, "I Must Be About My Father's Business."

Contemporary stained glass at St. Philip's Episcopal Church.

To see stained glass brought into the twenty-first century, look up to the twenty-foot-high window dominating the balcony. Designed in 2000 by Brooklyn artist James Best, the modern masterpiece was donated by Earl and Barbara Kydd Graves in memory of their parents. Graves is the much-heralded entrepreneur and publisher of *Black Enterprise* magazine, as well as a former parishioner. The window's central figure of the risen Christ hovering over a blue river seems to resemble the donor, a tradition dating to medieval churches. Contemporary disciples are represented by community members: the nurse with her Red Cross bag; an architect with rolled plans; a baseball player with his glove; an artist with easel and brushes; a farmer with his shovel; a businesswoman with her briefcase; and the scientist holding a beaker and test tubes. The merchant marine officer in military dress is a gracious tribute to Mrs. Graves's father.

The heritage of the present congregation is also celebrated by the Gilbert Montefiore Skeene Memorial window, which was installed in 1976 and honors Absalom Jones, dressed in nineteenth-century garb, who was ordained in Philadelphia as the first African American Episcopal priest in 1804. Local artist Jimmy James Greene's window from 1999 has worshipers carrying the Eucharistic offering of bread and wine.

An intimate chapel tucked alongside the main altar holds the columbarium. Three windows over its small altar, as well as an image of St. Peter with a fishing net, hold tiny icons of a white-robed monk that identifies the artistry of Whitefriars Glassworks in England. Visitors can enter during the week through the conference center at 270 Decatur Street.

334 MacDonough Street (between Lewis and Stuyvesant Avenues), Brooklyn, NY 11233; 718-778-8700

BY THE WAY

Nazarene Congregational United Church of Christ was founded in 1873 by the black Yale Divinity graduate Solomon Melvin Coles (1844–1924) for a black congregation. He served until 1877, when he left for Texas to continue ministering to black groups. The Gothic pale brick church played an active role in the struggle for social justice and sponsors popular lectures in its wood-filled sanctuary.

506 MacDonough Street (and Patchen Avenue), Brooklyn, NY 11233; 718-493-5995

BETHANY BAPTIST CHURCH

This sanctuary is located just outside the historic district of Stuyvesant Heights that was developed from 1870 to 1930 as an elite residential community. This congregation was organized in 1883 as the Messiah Mission, led by Reverend Joseph Bacon. Members relocated from Atlantic Avenue in 1924, but as the first black church in the area, they would not be welcomed by white residents.

The group purchased Trinity Baptist Church and grew to build the present Tudor-influenced sanctuary in 1967 under the leadership of Dr. William Augustus Jones Jr. The huge stone church sits on a corner site and has a modern interior filled with golden oak benches, a matching balcony and a wood-filled apse holding the stained-glass roundel of a red-robed Jesus nestled high above the baptismal pool. The narthex's art glass represents Jesus as the Lamb of God, along with the Lord's hand imparting a blessing, a reminder of the only accepted representation of the human body in Jewish temples.

460 Marcus Garvey Boulevard (between Decatur and MacDonough Streets), Brooklyn, NY 11216; 718-455-8400

MOUNT LEBANON BAPTIST CHURCH

This golden-brick Romanesque Revival sanctuary was built in 1894 as Embury Methodist Episcopal Church by the Parfitt brothers and purchased in 1948 by the present congregation. The members organized in 1905 under the guidance of Reverend Daniel W. Hill in Brownsville and would move many times before settling in Stuyvesant Heights.

Round towers with verdigris copper trim are topped by terra-cotta shingled roofs, while a textured arch entry leads into a cream-colored interior with seating for 1,200. Visit the small chapel that holds a culturally relevant stained-glass window of *The Last Supper*, along with a wood reredos gilded with the phrase, "Prayer Changes Things." An exterior sign on the chapel, opened daily from noon to 2:00 p.m., reminds neighbors, "Why Worry When You Can Pray."

230 Decatur Street (and Lewis Avenue), Brooklyn, NY 11233; 718-493-8770

FULTON PARK

This two-acre rectangle features the life-size sculpture of fashionably dressed inventor Robert Fulton (1765–1815), who leans on a model of his steamboat, the *Nassau*. His inventive ferry, traveling between Brooklyn and Manhattan, had an enormous impact on the growth of Long Island. An original zinc statue, designed in 1872 by Caspar Buberl, had been removed from the Old Fulton Ferry House and put into storage, only to be discovered in 1930. Today's bronze image sitting on a granite base was recast in 1955. This serene spot is located on Fulton Street between Lewis and Stuyvesant Avenues.

Also on Fulton Street is the Bedford-Stuyvesant Restoration Center, built in the 1970s and inspired by New York senators Robert F. Kennedy and Jacob Javits to promote urban renewal. It has funded the rehabilitation of hundreds of buildings in the area and revitalized the neighborhood. It is located at 1360 Fulton Street (718-636-3300).

Crown Heights

Legend has it that this area, infamous for its penitentiary, was called Crow Hill, and when development started, the jail was demolished and the region renamed for its initials: Crown Heights. Black residents have lived here since the 1600s, laboring on Dutch farms, while nearby communities of Weeksville and Carrsville prospered from the 1830s to the 1870s.

During the 1920s, European immigrants settled here, and in addition to the longstanding African American population, immigrants arrived in the 1950s from the Caribbean. Speaking English, Dutch, Spanish and French, they came from Haiti, Jamaica, Trinidad, Barbados and Grenada. Today, the largest group of Haitians in America resides in the community, and Caribbean heritage is celebrated with an annual Labor Day parade on Eastern Parkway. Sacred havens, numbering over forty-six, hold multilingual services.

Meanwhile, a substantial number of Orthodox Hasidim also work and live in the community. The Lubavitch sect emigrated from Russia after World War II and has worldwide headquarters on Eastern Parkway, along with many synagogues in traditional buildings and private homes.

THE WEEKSVILLE HOUSES
(HUNTERFLY ROAD HISTORIC HOUSES)

Four wood-frame cottages built from 1840 to 1883 hold the legacy of Weeksville, one of the oldest communities of freed slaves. Overshadowed by the huge Kingborough Housing Project, they were scheduled for the wrecking ball when community activists, led by Joan Maynard, saved the Hunterfly Road Historic Houses.

The landmark buildings were discovered in 1968 during an archaeological survey from the air by historian James Hurley and pilot Joseph Haynes. Old Hunterfly Road was a Native American trading route, as well as a path traveled by George Washington's soldiers in the Continental army. The road was not an official street and never appeared on the Brooklyn street grid, but it remained an important piece of American history.

James Weeks, a black longshoreman from Virginia, purchased farmland from the Lefferts family in 1838 and developed this unique homestead. Slavery had been prohibited in New York since 1827, but antiabolitionists and the later Draft Riots of the Civil War created a need for safe havens; many freed slaves moved near Weeks's farm for protection.

By the 1870s, several hundred residents had established schools, churches and businesses to become a self-reliant community. Susan Smith-McKinney-Steward (1847-1918), the first black female physician in New York State, was born in Weeksville, and her father, Sylvanus Smith, was a trustee of the African Free Schools of Brooklyn. Susan practiced medicine from her home at 178 Ryerson Street and is now eternally resting at Green-Wood Cemetery.

Weeksville became part of Crown Heights after the opening of the Brooklyn Bridge caused major demographic shifts in 1883. Large numbers of white Europeans moved to this green oasis.

1698 Bergen Street (between Buffalo and Rochester Avenues), Brooklyn, NY 11213; 718-756-5250

GRACE REFORMED CHURCH

Organized in 1858 by Gertrude Lefferts Vanderbilt as the Society for the Amelioration of the Colored Population of Flatbush, the church began as a children's Sunday school in a gardener's shed and evolved into Grace Chapel, a mission of the Flatbush Reformed Dutch Church. After its present sanctuary was built in 1893 by architect George T. Morse, the congregation was recognized as an independent church in 1903. Glorious stained-glass windows fill the sanctuary, with tributes to the Lefferts family, whose estate was divided in 1893, creating Lefferts Manor, zoned for private homes and allowing no commercial ventures.

1800 Bedford Avenue (and Lincoln Avenue), Brooklyn, NY 11225; 718-287-4343

By the Way

French-speaking Caribbean congregations have more than ten churches, including two on Rogers Avenue: Eglise Evangelique Church des Brooklyn at number 804 and Eglise du Nazarene Liberes at number 452. St. Francis of Assisi–St. Blaise at 319 Maple Street (718-756-2015) is a Roman Catholic congregation that was established in 1898. There are eight Baptist churches, including St. Mark's Baptist Church at 551 Rogers Avenue, which has a private school.

Bethel Tabernacle AME Church

When it was founded in 1847, the church site was part of Weeksville, which would be absorbed into Crown Heights. It was originally located across from its present location, but that sanctuary was demolished for a housing development in 1978. The congregation moved into a red brick schoolbuilding, NYC Public School 83, and adapted the space for worship, but the building came with an interesting history. In 1864, the white student body was merged with pupils from Colored School 2, which had been founded by original Weeksville residents.

90 Schenectady Avenue (between Troy and Dean Streets), Brooklyn, NY 11213; 718-221-2187

Our Lady of Charity Roman Catholic Church

An Italian immigrant congregation founded in 1903 built its first church in 1908 and worshipped in its own language. Today, this one-story modern brick and limestone church from 1952 is cared for by a black congregation.

In the interior apse, the stark image of the crucified Christ has been placed against the annotated map of Africa by James Maxwell. Altar cloths

The Black Madonna at Our Lady of Charity Church.

are designed with culturally relevant motifs, while artist Tucker Wallace enhanced the baptismal niche with the Black Madonna, who is surrounded by Reverend Martin Luther King Jr., Malcolm X, Sojourner Truth and Harriet Tubman.

In 1974, the first black pastor, Reverend James Goode, OFM, revitalized the congregation and commissioned the relevant artwork for the nave. He was also founder of the National Black Catholic Apostolate, a ministry with African American families that, Goode noted, "walks in the footsteps of St. Francis of Assisi who stands up for human dignity and restores hope to the community." Today, Solid Ground Ministry, sponsored by the Franciscan Order, is the new name for Goode's idea, which evolved into a national movement. Look on the exterior façade for Mary holding her infant son, Jesus, both regally dressed to reflect the style of the founding Italian congregation.

1669 Dean Street (between Utica and Schenectady Avenues), Brooklyn, NY 11213; 718-774-5100

BEREAN MISSIONARY BAPTIST CHURCH

Located up the street from the Weeksville Houses, this church was organized in about 1851 by a racially mixed congregation that chose its name from the Bible. Berea, a fertile site about fifteen miles north of Jerusalem, was conquered by the Israelites. Reverend Daniel Resse, a white minister and abolitionist, led the group, but it split over the church's location on a high hill that was difficult to navigate.

On part of its site, the congregation had erected a Romanesque brownstone church in 1898, with castle-like turrets and an engraved lintel bearing its name. That building remains on the property and is utilized for social programs. Today's services are held in a huge modern red brick annex built in 1960. The interior nave is surrounded by a wood-faced balcony and focuses on an immense stained-glass window above the choir stalls and the pastor's pulpit. Besides caring for spiritual needs, the church sponsors wellness programs for adults and children in its family health center.

Two other Baptist churches evolved from this group: Cornerstone Baptist, founded in 1917 and residing since 1944 in the former Lewis Avenue Congregational Church at 562 Madison Avenue (718-574-5900), and Brown Memorial Baptist Church in Clinton Hill (see entry).

1635 Bergen Street (between Rochester and Utica Avenues), Brooklyn, NY 11213; 718-774-0466

St. Gregory the Great

This Roman Catholic Irish and Italian congregation, founded in 1906 by Monsignor Maurice Fitzgerald, dedicated its second structure, designed by Helmle & Corbett, in 1916. It is an architectural gem inspired by fifth-century Roman churches and has been admired as one of the most impressive sanctuaries in Brooklyn.

The Roman basilica design in white pressed brick with terra-cotta trim is enhanced with a decorative bell tower rising seven stories alongside an exterior wall; it was a gift from the Carberry Sisters in 1931. An impressive porch is lined with Ionic columns, while the wheel window by J.G. Guthrie and niches holding the four evangelists (Matthew, Mark, Luke and John) adorn the firty-foot-wide exterior.

The warmth of the interior is augmented by a dark wood ceiling with stenciled rafters, one reading "O How Lovely Is Your Dwelling Place." Above the main altar, a huge mural tells the story of Pope Gregory (circa 540–604) sending Augustine of Canterbury with a group of monks to tend to the conversion of Great Britain in AD 596. Gregory, a Benedictine monk and author, became pope in 590 when war, famine and plague swept through Rome. His creation, the vocal musical form called Gregorian chant, remains an intricate part of church ritual.

In 1991, a portrait of St. Martin de Porres, a black lay brother from the Dominican Friary in Lima, Peru, who was admired for his humility, was donated by local artist Doctor Appah. The large Caribbean congregation arrived in the 1960s, joining African American members from the 1950s.

224 Brooklyn Avenue (between St. John's and Sterling Place), Brooklyn, NY 11213; 718-773-0100

ST. MARK'S EPISCOPAL CHURCH

This was the first Episcopal parish organized in 1837, in the city of Williamsburg. As the congregation grew, it was able to build its first church in 1841 at Bedford Avenue and South Fifth Street, but in 1896, the property was taken as eminent domain to build the Williamsburg Bridge approach. The group relocated to its present site and first erected a large Gothic parish house in 1901, with a chapel and school, designed by Henry M. Congdon & Son. The house was renovated with a new façade and tower in 1937, but the planned church was never built.

In 1958, the St. Mark's white congregation merged with St. Timothy's black members, whose church had closed, creating a more vibrant community. West Indian newcomers joined in the 1960s, and today, the sanctuary has more than three thousand Caribbean immigrants in its congregation. Look for stained-glass windows (installed in 1974) that honor American history makers Reverend Martin Luther King Jr., Marcus Garvey, Harriet Taubman and the educator Mary McLeod Bethune.

1417 Union Street (between Brooklyn and Kingston Avenues), Brooklyn, NY 11213; 718-756-6607

BROOKLYN JEWISH CENTER (OHOLEI TORAH INSTITUTE)

After World War I, this vibrant center was the pride of American Jewry and the focus for the community lead by Rabbi Israel H. Levinthal. The building included an elaborate synagogue, a ballroom, a day school, a kosher restaurant and a health club. Founded in 1919 and built in 1922 by Louis A. Abramson with Margon & Glasser, this Neoclassical building's huge sanctuary was filled with eleven stained-glass windows. During the 1950s, demographics started to shift, but the Conservative congregation held on until 1985, when it agreed to sell the building to the Lubavitch Hasidim sect, to be used as an educational institution, Oholei Torah (Tent of Torah). The center's records from 1921 to 1985 were sent to the Jewish Theological Seminary and are filled with prominent names: Rubin (Richard) Tucker from the Metropolitan Opera as cantor, Albert Einstein as guest speaker and Broadway's Moss Hart as social director.

PART III

Since education was an important goal for the founding congregation, it is fitting that the center remained a teaching institute.

667 Eastern Parkway (New York and Brooklyn Avenues), Brooklyn, NY 11213; 718-483-9000

CONGREGATION LUBAVITCH

The Lubavitch sect, with its name derived from the town of Lubavitch in Lithuania, is the only Hasidic group in the community. The European sect was begun in 1788 by Rabbi Schneur Zalman of Liadi and remains centered on a charismatic leader. In the 1940s, many followers arrived in Brooklyn and organized hundreds of congregations, each consisting of ten to fifteen people. The members purchased their Tudor-styled building from a medical clinic to become a home for their leader, Rabbi Yoseph Yitzchak Schneerson, who managed to escape Nazi persecution. The site, expanded with two additions in the 1960s and '70s, functions as worldwide headquarters, with an impressive library of rare books in Hebrew and Yiddish that opened in 1992.

This is the only Hasidic group that proselytizes with handouts and amplified sound trucks, and it can be seen and heard in the city's busiest areas and on college campuses. Men pray three times a day and require ten adult males for a minyan (prayer group). They continue to wear the black garb, beard and peyos (uncut forelocks) like early ancestors, and they are the only Hasidic sect whose members speak English as their main language. Women, dressing modestly, cannot hold any leadership positions or drive vehicles, and their marriages are arranged.

Rabbi Menachem Mendel Schneerson, who died in 1994, was the seventh and last rabbi and expanded the congregation to a worldwide movement by emphasizing Torah study and canvassing among secular Jews. Currently, the group has appointed a mashpia (inspirer) as leader, with all policies, guidelines and finances determined by a small group of rabbis. Conflict has arisen concerning the late rabbi, whom many believed to be the Messiah, and the debate continues to unsettle the community. With more than twenty schools and many chapels in private homes, there is sometimes a need to utilize public streets for overflow when celebrating special occasions.

770 Eastern Parkway, Brooklyn, NY 11213; 718-774-4000

Brownsville and East New York

In 1865, Charles S. Brown successfully marketed the development of his purchased farmland into a middle-class suburb. Located in mid-eastern Brooklyn, the region was not easily accessible until the Fulton Street elevated train arrived in 1889, and the Williamsburg Bridge transported workers in 1903.

By the 1920s, the area had become so heavily populated with Jewish immigrants from eastern Europe and Lower Manhattan that it was known as the "Jerusalem of America." Poet Emma Lazarus (1849–1887) was born and died in the community and is most famous for "The New Colossus," with her words immortalized on the base of the Statue of Liberty: "Give me your tired, your poor, your huddled masses yearning to breathe free." The words seem an echo of what Jewish residents found in Brownsville.

Margaret Sanger, who belonged to active reform circles, opened the first American birth control clinic in 1916 on Amboy Street. In the 1930s, Italian immigrants settled in its northern section, but like many neighborhoods following World War II, they would move south to greener pastures. During the 1960s, an influx of black residents from downtown Brooklyn, Harlem and the Caribbean reversed the demographics, and public housing projects saturated the area. The Council of East Brooklyn Churches took an active role in revitalizing the community in the 1980s, and Caribbean immigrants continued to arrive, bringing new vitality to the area. More than forty-four sacred havens are found in the neighborhood, and they remain an important source of history. Some Jewish symbols are still found on former synagogues and façades of commercial buildings.

ZION TRIANGLE PARK

Peter Vandeveer, for whom the park was first named, donated the tract of land in 1896, but in recognition of the local Jewish population, the park was renamed in 1911. Once the gathering spot for local anarchists and public debates, it holds the Brownsville War Memorial by Charles C. Rumsey, dedicated in 1925 to honor those who died in World War I. A bas-relief image of the sword-bearing *Winged Victory* is accompanied by the local boys' names. Look for the Shield of David engraved on squat pylons bordering the stairway. It is located at Pitkin and East New York Avenues.

BROWNSVILLE COMMUNITY BAPTIST CHURCH

Since each church is run autonomously with no hierarchy, there was an enormous growth of Baptist churches throughout Brooklyn. As one of Brownsville's eight Baptist churches, this congregation was organized in 1971 within the boundaries of Tilden Houses, the public housing complex built in 1961 on more than ten acres and named for New York governor Samuel Tilden (1814–1886).

The modern light brick building has an enclosed portico leading into the two-story sanctuary. Huge, clear glass rounded-arch windows fill the serene white interior with glorious light. The denomination baptizes by total immersion, so the sanctuary pool has a prominent position in front of the nave. It is located at 600 Mother Gaston Boulevard (between Stone and Dumont Avenues), Brooklyn, New York, 11212 (718-342-3637).

Neighbors include First Baptist Church at 357 Chester Avenue (718-498-1074) and People's Baptist Church at 105 Riverdale Avenue (718-345-6587).

BY THE WAY

Our Lady of Mercy Roman Catholic Church was organized in 1961 for the local African American and Caribbean populations and was among the founding members of East Brooklyn Churches, which worked with the community's poverty and housing programs. The small, modern red brick sanctuary is filled with abstract stained-glass windows and diminutive wooden figures on cream-colored walls that effectively depict the Stations of the Cross. Members of the "Garifuna Legacy," representing migrants and descendants from Honduras, Nicaragua, Guatemala and Belize, also celebrate at the church with culturally relevant services and music. It is located at 680 Mother Gaston Boulevard (between Riverdale and Livonia Avenues), Brooklyn, New York, 11212 (718-346-3166).

Brownsville AME Zion Church is part of the African Methodist Episcopal Zion Conference of Churches, organized in 1820 and which spread throughout the United States and Canada. It is located at 1696 East New York Avenue (718-496-8062).

Universal Temple Church of God, a Christian house of worship, resides in the former synagogue of Congregation Adath Yeshurun, with the Shield of David still high on the exterior façade. It is located at 1403 Eastern Parkway, Brooklyn, New York, 11233 (718-774-5725).

In the 1980s, the East Brooklyn Congregations, a group of fifty church leaders from varied sects, developed a strategy to save their devastated neighborhood. While crime was an issue, the lack of good housing was overwhelming. Mayor Edward Koch was approached with a proposal to offer low-cost vacant land, and church leaders would pledge the necessary funds to build affordable homes.

What evolved was the Nehemiah Plan, named for the Old Testament prophet sent to Jerusalem to help rebuild that city; it would develop more than 2,500 homes in East New York and Brownsville. Nearby, Mother Gaston Boulevard (formerly Stone Avenue) honors Rosetta Gaston (1885–1981), a resident and self-taught historian and founder of the Brownsville Heritage House for educational and cultural development (581 Mother Gaston Boulevard). Because of her loving nature, she was called "Mother" by her admirers. See the Mother Gaston bronze statue at Dumont Avenue. The neighborhood is also spiritually alive, claiming more than eighty-five churches.

ST. PAUL'S COMMUNITY BAPTIST CHURCH

Reverend Johnny Ray Youngblood focused on a socially relevant ministry and built this sanctuary into a thriving center for social justice. Arriving in 1974 and retiring in 2009, Youngblood left the legacy safe in the hands of his former associate, Pastor David K. Brawley.

The church began as a storefront chapel in 1927, with 15 members lead by Reverend S.V. Reeves. In the 1940s, they built a sanctuary only to see it demolished for urban renewal. Today's beige brick church was built as Congregation B'nai Israel in the 1960s and purchased by St. Paul's in 1979; it has been refitted by the congregation to seat about 1,200 worshipers. The large narthex accommodates the crowds arriving for services in an enhanced sanctuary filled with grand skylights in the wood-beam ceiling.

For two weeks in September, the church sponsors the annual commemoration of the Maafa (Swahili for "great suffering and disaster"), when members reenact the grief of families torn apart by the slave trade. Inner strength to overcome injustice is reinforced by dancers and drummers joining in *The Maafa Suite*, with a memorable finale held on a nearby beach, not unlike the ports from which slave ships sailed.

St. Paul's is named for the apostle whose well-known legacy is the record of his missionary adventures, much like the former pastor's legacy of establishing outreach programs and a private school system and as cochair of the Nehemiah Program, which helped rebuild East New York and Brownsville.

859 Hendrix Street (between Linden Boulevard and Stanley Avenue), Brooklyn, NY 11207; 718-257-1300

New Lots Community Church

Looking like it belongs on a country lane, this white wood landmark church was built in 1821 by local Dutch farmers, who cut the oak timbers and used pegs to fasten the joints together. Three windows above three doors, all with early Gothic arches, are topped by a low-gabled roof. Look up to see the charming octagonal bell tower and marvel how this well-crafted haven survived.

The area was originally called Ostwont (Dutch for "East Woods") in the 1670s, until Flatbush farmers relocated to another land tract and named it New Lots to differentiate from the Flatbush village center of Old Lots. The rural area's name was again changed in 1835 when John Pitkin purchased land north of New Lots Avenue and called it East New York, since it was at the eastern end of New York City.

653 Schenck Avenue (and New Lots Avenue), Brooklyn, NY 11207; 718-257-3455

By the Way

Holy Trinity Russian Orthodox Church was organized in 1909 by Belorussian immigrants who built their red brick and copper-domed sanctuary in 1935. Although the congregation is small, newly arriving Russian immigrants are revitalizing the church.

400 Glenmore Avenue (and Pennsylvania Avenue), Brooklyn, NY 11207; 718-498-0518

Bushwick

In 1660, Peter Stuyvesant, the director-general of New Amsterdam, permitted French settlers to establish a town in the northwest section of Brooklyn that now includes Williamsburg and Greenpoint. The town's name was derived from the Dutch word *boswyck* ("little town in the woods"); the British called it Bushwick Green. The area evolved from farmland to breweries when German immigrants arrived in the 1840s, and an elevated train line opened a new link to Manhattan in 1885. Italian immigrants took over the German enclave in the 1940s, and nearly 80 percent of the population today is Hispanic.

Bushwick lists more than eighty sacred havens in a neighborhood that shares a fluid border with Bedford-Stuyvesant, Williamsburg and, to the north, Ridgewood, Queens. In 1973, the Better Living Ecumenical Realty Center was founded by six churches to rehabilitate housing, but drug traffic was rampant and progress slow. Today, young professionals and artists from Williamsburg are flowing into Bushwick due to affordable housing and good access to public transportation. Stately mansions still remain from the German brewers and prosperous businessmen, as do the many sacred havens that keep Bushwick's history alive for another generation.

Maria Hernandez Park

This six-acre grassland established in 1896 and known as Bushwick Park was renamed in 1989 for Maria Hernandez (1953–1989). She lived in Bushwick and fought along with her husband and neighbors against the community's epidemic of drug dealers. Maria was killed in her home by gunshots fired through her window and is fittingly remembered in this peaceful haven for her courage and determination. It is located at Irving and Knickerbocker Avenues (between Starr and Suydam Streets).

Reformed Church of South Bushwick

As recorded in church archives, the landmark wood-frame church, dedicated in 1853, was designed in Greek Revival style by the Messiers Morgan. The two-story white church is capped with an octagonal tower and steeple, while Ionic columns with impressive capitals frame the portico's entrance door; additional wings were added in 1883.

Families from twenty neighboring farms started this parish in 1851 on property donated by members Abraham and Andrew Stockholm and were assisted by a grant from the Collegiate Church of New York. Most of these Dutch families were descendants of the Old Bushwick Reform Church dating from 1654. The green garden that surrounds the sanctuary is a visual reminder of this once rural neighborhood, and note also the adjacent avenue named for the church's first pastor, John Himrod.

855–67 Bushwick and Himrod Avenues, Brooklyn, NY 11221; 718-452-3326

Church of St. Barbara

Elaborate twin towers highlight the Spanish Baroque church designed in 1910 by Helmle & Huberty. The building is named for two Barbaras: one a sainted martyr beheaded by her father for converting to Christianity, and the other a daughter of local German brewer and church patron Leonard Eppig. This Roman Catholic congregation, founded in 1893, was part of the large German community that had first built the nearby St. Leonard's Church in 1871. It was demolished in 2001, and records were transferred to

St. Joseph's Universal Church on Suydam Street, which had opened in 1919 for Italian immigrants.

The handsome beige and white exterior has round arches, niches and towers that soar more than 140 feet, while a decorative interior extends 170 feet and is lined with marble columns holding sculptures of the apostles (a German trademark). An ornate barrel-vaulted nave is richly ornamented with framed biblical paintings from the Old Testament. Look for Adam and Eve forced from the Garden of Eden; Melchisedek, ancient priest and king of Jerusalem; and the first Passover, as told in Exodus. Today, the church tends to the needs of its Hispanic congregation.

138 Bleecker Street (and Central Avenue), Brooklyn, NY 11221; 718-452-3660

OUR LADY OF GOOD COUNSEL

This Roman Catholic German and Irish congregation was founded in 1886 on what was then identified as the border of affluent Bedford-Stuyvesant. The members built the gray granite Gothic church with an asymmetrical tower in 1890 and filled the sanctuary with stained glass from Germany and tile floors from Spain. It would feel the effects of urban decay when former members moved on to greener pastures.

In 1976, the dormant bell tower was brought back to life by Reverend Vincent Gallo and a team of volunteers. The rebirth echoed the rebuilding of the community, and the pastor proclaimed, "Bells are an echo of the voice of God." Edgar Allan Poe (1809–1849), famous for his own poetic bells, wrote a little-known poem, *Catholic Hymn*, seemingly to ring out his own rebirth: "At morn—at noon—at twilight dim/ Maria! Thou hast heard my hymn!" Poe was not unlike today's immigrants, whose lives are filled with hardships, but they have this sanctuary to assist with social problems and spiritual nourishment. It is located at 915 Putnam Avenue, Brooklyn, New York, 11221 (718-443-7211).

Meanwhile, St. John the Baptist Roman Catholic Church, the massive Romanesque basilica built in 1894 by Patrick Keely, is now the administrative office for Our Lady of Good Counsel. It is located at 75 Lewis Avenue, between Hart Street and Willoughby Avenue (718-455-6864).

PART III

BY THE WAY

On Putnam Avenue, visit St. Leonard's Afro-American Orthodox Church at number 765; it was built in 1909 as a synagogue for Congregation Shaari Zedek and purchased by the congregation in 1944 (718-452-0580).

Old Mount Zion Baptist Church is at number 894 (718-574-4811).

Bushwick Avenue is home to Bushwick United Methodist Church at number 1139 (718-574-6610), and Mount of Olives Seventh-Day Adventist is at number 975 (718-453-6312).

Evergreen Avenue is also spiritually alive with Christ Temple Pentecostal Church at number 390 (718-452-0621).

Evergreen Baptist Church is at number 455 (718-574-5854), and Iglesia de Dios Pentacostal Rey de Gloria is at number 465, one of many small chapels caring for the Hispanic community.

Williamsburg

In 1802, Richard Woodhull introduced his new ferry line to carry farm produce across the East River to Manhattan, all the while thinking of creating a village honoring Jonathan Williams, the original surveyor of this part of Bushwick. Woodhull went bankrupt, but David Dunham, who introduced a steam ferry, saw the dream become reality when the community was incorporated in 1827 and became a destination for commerce. Many say that the real magnet was the Noah Waterbury Distillery, which was opened in 1819. Shoreline industries employed workers as shipbuilders, brewers, laborers at sugar refineries and associates with the Charles Pratt, Corning Glass and Charles Pfizer companies.

The region first welcomed wealthier families who employed architects to design fashionable homes, followed by a massive influx of German and Irish immigrants who built smaller residences. All planned sacred havens for their enclaves.

The population grew so large that Williamsburgh became a city in 1852. The Italian community that arrived in the 1880s grew so huge that it flowed into Greenpoint and south to Bensonhurst. When the area was incorporated into the city of Brooklyn in 1855, it dropped the final "h" in its name, but the spelling remains in the neighborhood.

Williamsburg Bridge (see Downtown Brooklyn), completed in 1903, attracted poorer immigrants to flee Lower Manhattan and flock to suburban pastures. Orthodox Jews could also continue traditions of shtetl life in dress and rituals while returning on the bridge's pedestrian path for supplies on

Manhattan's Orchard and Delancey Streets. Construction of tenements was started to house the newcomers, and in 1938, the first public housing complex was built.

The Jewish group of Satmar Hasidim arrived in the 1940s following World War II and grew dramatically. Beginning in the 1950s, the construction of the Brooklyn-Queens Expressway (BQE) sliced up streets, erecting concrete barriers through neighborhood avenues, demolishing homes and sanctuaries and physically dividing the north and south sides of Williamsburg. In the 1960s, housing projects were built on the east side, causing the demolition of hundreds of homes and businesses.

Along with the Hasidim, Puerto Rican immigrants in the 1950s settled on the south side, calling it Los Sures. The north side remains filled with Italian and Polish descendants, joined by another layer of diversity—young families and hip artists who discovered the ambience of a small village with convenient access to Manhattan.

Ethnic designations can still be found engraved on spiritual places, testifying to the fact that foreign language–speaking immigrants segregated themselves in their cultural homes. More than forty-two sacred havens include many Hispanic congregations, plus four public synagogues and too many to count in private homes. The proliferation of Roman Catholic churches reflects the Irish, German and Italian majority that once settled in the neighborhood. Street names honor fifty-six delegates who signed the Declaration of Independence.

HOLY TRINITY CATHEDRAL OF THE UKRAINIAN ORTHODOX CHURCH

Located near the equestrian statue of George Washington at Valley Forge, this opulent Christian cathedral was once the branch of Williamsburgh Trust Company, which retains its identity with three sculptured bank seals on the façade. Due to convenient exits from the bridge, the area became a major banking hub, with remnants of its past still evident: the landmark Williamsburgh Savings Bank from 1870 retains its handsome round dome with golden weather-vane and is about to become a private events space; Kings County Savings Bank, built in 1868, is now an art and cultural center; and Dime Savings Bank from 1864 remains in business.

The triple bar liturgical cross that crowns the dome of Holy Trinity Cathedral identifies the former bank as a place of worship for Eastern

Holy Trinity Cathedral of the Ukrainian Orthodox Church.

Orthodox congregations. The building had been abandoned in 1911, becoming a courthouse in 1928 and finally being purchased by the Ukrainian Church in 1961. This glistening, white Roman Revival sanctuary with a central dome, Ionic columns and terra-cotta façade was designed by Helmle & Huberty in 1906. Its powerful exterior has stood the test of time, while the walls within bear no evidence of its former life. The decorative interior of sky blue and cream has been adapted to liturgical needs with the installation of a towering iconostatis, an altar screen filled with gilded-framed icons and an entrance to the sacred altar. The sanctuary's biblical murals, golden chandeliers and stained-glass windows glow with light filtered through the clear glass dome, as well as from dozens of cream-colored candles.

185 South 5th Street (and New Street), Brooklyn, NY 11211, 718-388-4723

St. Paul's Lutheran Church

This Romanesque Revival red brick church, with its enormous tower, sits grandly on a busy corner site between the Brooklyn-Queens Expressway and the elevated subway line on Broadway, almost as a reminder that it just missed the wrecking ball of progress. Now serving the neighborhood's Hispanic and English congregations, the landmark church was founded in 1853 by German immigrants who built the present sanctuary designed by J.C. Cady in 1884. The church's round-arch design, known as *rundbogenstil*, was brought to America by the German congregation, which favored this style for its second site. With its German name inscribed over the side door, the building represents the huge population that established local businesses, waterfront industries, cultural centers and the German Savings Bank in 1866.

Rich Black Forest wood creates the interior's timbered ceiling, the apse's reredos and the three-sided curved balcony. A unique slim brass baptismal font, donated in 1916 by Herman and Wilhelmina Schomaker, is tucked into the front of the sanctuary. Stenciled and softly stained art glass works fill the leaded windows, while three figurative images of Jesus add vibrant color. Look in the balcony for the tripartite Tiffany window *The Agony in the Garden*, portraying the kneeling Christ praying on the Mount of Olives before his death.

While the interior holds no visual reference to its patron, the sanctuary itself reflects Paul's Epistles and the Acts of the Apostles in the New Testament, for Lutheran teachings focus on Christianity as taught in the Bible by prophets and apostles. The sect evolved from the German Reformation, started by Martin Luther and Philip Melanchthon, the scholar who wrote *Augsburg Confession* in 1530 to explain to their king, Charles V, the ninety-five theses authored by Luther. Space is now shared with the Resurrection Presbyterian congregation in the true neighborly spirit of the community.

334 South 5th Street (and Marcy Avenue), Brooklyn, NY 11211; 718-782-1486

Sts. Peter and Paul Roman Catholic Church

Founded in 1843 as St. Mary's Roman Catholic Church on North 9th Street, the congregation had members scattered throughout the village. Reverend Sylvester Malone (1821–1899), a young Irish priest sent to build this parish, relocated the sanctuary in 1848 to its present site. He renamed the new endeavor for two of the followers of Jesus and served his entire life in a parish that he would see divided twenty-five times, as the continuous influx of immigrants necessitated additional sanctuaries. As well as ministering to huge congregations, the charismatic pastor worked with architect Patrick Keely (1816–1896) to build the first Gothic church that Keely designed for the Diocese of New York. Utilized from 1848 to 1957, the sanctuary was demolished, and the artifacts that Keely had carved with his carpentry skills were lost. Keely, who lived on Clermont Avenue in Fort Greene, was buried from this church and interred at Holy Cross Cemetery.

Archival records show that Father Malone crusaded for social justice, interacted with politicians, created a church library and book club and was the best-known priest in Brooklyn. He was also a member of the Academia, a group of liberal clergy often in conflict with the bishop. Today's modern brick church, with images of its patrons on the interior's reredos, serves neighborhood Hispanic and English members.

71 South 3rd Street (between Berry and Wythe Avenues), Brooklyn, NY 11211; 718-388-9576

EPIPHANY ROMAN CATHOLIC CHURCH

Originally built as All Souls Universalist Church in 1874 by James Rodwell, this Romanesque red brick design has retained original stained glass, symmetrical twin towers and two sets of entrance doors with round terra-cotta arches. The sanctuary was purchased in 1905 by the archdiocese for the neighborhood's growing Irish congregation. The interior nave was altered in the 1960s, and a dropped ceiling was added to conserve heating fuel. Look up and imagine what's waiting to be uncovered.

96 South 9th Street (between Bedford and Berry Streets), Brooklyn, NY 11211; 718-387-6328

IGLESIA CRISTIANA PENTECOSTAL LA LUZ DEL MUNDO (LIGHT OF THE WORLD CHRISTIAN PENTECOSTAL CHURCH)

Thomas W. Little designed this wide Italianate sanctuary in 1853 for the New England Congregational Church. This sect, first established in New England in 1738, was run as a society of Christian families with a pastor and deacons but no hierarchy; each church was run independently, and all worked together for the common good. Transplanted New Englanders first built Plymouth Church (see Brooklyn Heights) in 1847 and attracted well-educated churchgoers from many other sects, and this led to the rapid expansion of the Congregational community.

Services at La Luz del Mundo.

Listed as the oldest landmark in Williamsburg, the popular church was destroyed by fire in 1893 and rebuilt in 1894 with a wide-open auditorium-style nave. Exterior triangular pediments over two entrances and three window units echo the roofline, while persimmon-trimmed round-arch windows contrast dramatically against brownstone walls. An exterior plaque details historical data, including the church's restoration in 2001.

In 1955, the present congregation moved into the spacious sanctuary, which seats 1,500. Double-tiered wood-faced galleries can be put to use when needed but are now utilized for video recordings of the music-filled services. Huge wood-encased organ pipes rest above a wood reredos on the center platform that holds the pastor's pulpit. Colorful national flags lining both sides of the sanctuary represent member countries, while golden stained-glass windows and a center dome with creamy milk-colored glass add refined light to the regal interior.

The narthex has a small chapel, original wooden staircases and stained-glass door panels as a reminder of the building's age. Church members are part of the Pentecostal movement, which began in about 1900 in the American South, and enjoy song, music and powerful preaching during joyful services.

176 South 9th Street (between Driggs and Roebling Avenues), Brooklyn, NY 11211; 718-384-8094

IGLESIA: ON THE SOUTH SIDE

With so many Spanish-speaking immigrants in the neighborhood, walk across any street, and you'll find storefront chapels or small buildings housing independent congregations. On South 2nd Street and Havemeyer, look for Iglesia Cristiana Mission Sin Fronteras (Mission Without Boundaries). Roca Eterna Pentecostal Church is at 248 Havemeyer and 2nd Street, and the Spanish Free Methodist Church at number 157 has its former name, Washington Palace, engraved above the entrance.

MOST HOLY TRINITY ROMAN CATHOLIC CHURCH

In 1841, a small wooden church was built on hilly farmland purchased from Abraham Meserole by founding pastor John Stephen Raffeiner, and in 1885, this Neo-Gothic stone church with huge twin spires tapering to 250 feet reflected the growth of the German congregation. Designed by William Schickel (1859–1907), who is remembered in the stained-glass window of St. Dominic, the sanctuary measures 170 feet in length and 82 feet in width. The majestic interior is filled with biblical murals painted by Wilhelm Lamprecht, Austrian windows by the Albert Neuhauser Company and an oak pulpit designed by the architect.

Symbols of the four evangelists are featured in the rose window, and read the names of generous German donors in the arcade's windows while imagining the congregation's pride when its new church opened. The founding pastor and his successor, Father Michael May, are resting eternally in the crypt below the sanctuary.

Polish immigrants have now joined Hispanic and African American members in continuing the vision of the founding congregation. Neighbors say that the movie version of *A Tree Grows in Brooklyn*, written by native Betty Smith, was filmed nearby on Maujer Street and Manhattan Avenue and represents the resilient nature of the community.

138 Montrose Street (between Manhattan and Graham Avenues), Brooklyn, NY 11206; 718-384-0215

ALL SAINTS

This Roman Catholic congregation, founded in 1866 by the German farming community with workers from the Navy Yard and local breweries, built its first church on this site and included an orphanage to address one of the pressing social problems of the day. The *Brooklyn Eagle* reported that four bishops dedicated the present sanctuary in the crowded neighborhood on November 26, 1896. The red brick Gothic church, with limestone, terra-cotta tracery and columns, was designed by Schickel and Ditmars. A serene cruciform interior, seating 1,500 and running 146 feet in length, glows with stained-glass windows by Mayer of Munich, elaborate Italian marble altars and green marble columns in the apse.

In 1904, when the Brookyn Bridge opened, the area experienced major population shifts. Congregations, which built these huge churches for posterity, could never have foreseen families leaving the neighborhood. After 1938, Italian immigrants became the dominant church group, but they were uprooted by public housing projects that demolished many homes in the 1960s. Today, Mexican and other Latin Americans have brought new rituals to the church and celebrate their patron Mary under the title of Our Lady of Guadalupe during street festivals.

115 Throop Avenue (between Flatbush Avenue and Thornton Street), Brooklyn, NY 11206; 718-388-1951

BY THE WAY

Testifying to the huge numbers of Catholic immigrants, large churches continued to fill the neighborhood. St. Nicholas, founded in 1865, now ministers to a Hispanic congregation in its red brick Gothic sanctuary with center tower built for German worshipers at 26 Olive Street and Powers Street (718-388-1420).

Transfiguration was founded in 1874 for Germans, who dedicated the present church in 1889. The huge stone sanctuary features the *rundbogenstil* (round arch) style that was popular with the community. See stained-glass windows from 1910, especially the transfiguration of Christ with Moses and Elijah, accompanied by apostles Peter, James and John on Mount Tabor. It is located at 263 Marcy Avenue and Hooper Street (718-388-8773).

BNOS YAKOV OF PUPA

This four-story Gothic building with pitched roof and squat tower now belongs to the Pupa Hasidim sect, whose name translates to "Daughters of Jacob," from the town of Pupa, Hungary. Like all Hasidim, this group is named after its town of origin.

The sanctuary was built as Temple Beth Elohim by Williamsburg's first congregation of German Jewish immigrants, founded in 1848. The group evolved into Union Reform Temple in Prospect Heights (see chapter). Prominently carved on its painted brownstone façade is the opening date of the synagogue, 1876, along with handsome exterior features such as a huge terra-cotta arch holding three lancet windows, the tympanum filled with multicolored tiles and two banded-arch entranceways.

Besides the Pupa, the neighborhood has concentrated areas of other Hasidim sects, including Satmar, Ger, Viznitz, Belz, Skver, Spinka, Breslov, Rachmastrivk and Toldos Aharon. A Keap Street lamppost holds the street sign subtitled "Rebbe Joel Teitelbaum Way," a tribute to the Satmar Hasidim founding leader.

274 Keap Street (between Marcy and Division Avenues), Brooklyn, NY; 718-963-1212

Bnos Yakov of Pupa.

CONGREGATION YETEV LEV D'SATMAR

This Satmar sect of Orthodox Judaism began in eastern Europe in the eighteenth century and takes its name from the town of Satmar, Hungary, where Rabbi Joel Teitelbaum fled when anti-Semitic policies began to be enforced preceding World War II. After several moves, he settled in Williamsburg in 1947, with his congregation revering him as a powerful spiritual leader. Kiryat Joel ("Joel's Town") was started upstate in Monroe, New York, in the 1970s and was also the final resting spot for the late rabbi. His two grandnephews, Aaron and Zalman, sons of Moses Teitelbaum, who succeeded Joel as the Satmar leader, lead their own groups, one in Brooklyn and the other upstate in Kiryat Joel.

Satmars discourage converts to Judaism but welcome back those who have strayed. They await the Messiah to redeem them, oppose creation of the modern state of Israel and consult their rabbi on all personal and business matters. Many synagogues are in private homes, and some are in public buildings, but all are within mandatory walking distances. Orthodox ritual does not allow members to carry anything from home to a public area during the Sabbath (sundown Friday to sundown Saturday), necessitating approved areas, called "eruvs," to be marked by wires strung on high poles. Women never mingle with men in public ceremonies and must cover their heads with wigs or scarves. Marriages are arranged, community involvement is restricted to the sect and children are educated in the Satmar school system. Rejecting the secular world, the sect is based on a fundamentalist belief that scripture is the revealed word of God and remains isolated from modern communication tools.

When you visit, you will find local streets filled with schoolchildren from the local yeshivas, mothers with strollers, men wearing eighteenth-century black ensembles and matzo bakeries. This close-knit community was depicted in the novel *The Chosen* by Chaim Potok, who exposed the human struggle between religion and the secular world.

152 Rodney Street, Brooklyn, NY 11211; 718-782-2342

BY THE WAY

Annunciation Roman Catholic Church placed in its exterior garden tall, free-standing wooden carvings of a cross and an image of the suffering Christ, reflecting traditions of the Lithuanian congregation, which arrived after 1914, as well as the Hispanic group that joined in the 1980s. Founded in 1863 by a German congregation, the red brick Romanesque church with handsome stone inlays emphasizing its rounded arches was built in 1870 by F.J. Berlenbach Jr. It is located at 259 North Fifth Street (and Havemeyer Street), Brooklyn, New York, 11211 (718-387-2111).

Holy Ghost Ukrainian Catholic Church was established in 1913 for Ukrainian immigrants, and today, second and third generations from original founders are joined by recent Ukrainian immigrants. This golden-brick sanctuary's limestone portal holds the tripartite arched entry with a copper-trimmed triangular pediment. It features a pastel mosaic panel with the image of the Holy Spirit in the form of a white dove and two guardian angels. The warm interior has a stenciled border around the nave, while the apse is filled with iconic murals. Services are held in the native language. It is located at 161 North 5th Street (between Bedford and Driggs Avenues), Brooklyn, New York, 11211 (718-782-9592).

Iglesia Bautista Hispana Calvario, Spanish Baptists, worship in the Romanesque Revival red brick sanctuary built in 1864 for the German congregation of St. Matthew's Lutheran Church. Over time, the interior and exterior have been severely altered, but look along side walls to see the brick buttresses, the reason for the building's longevity. It is located at 201 North 5th Street (between Reobling and Driggs), Brooklyn, New York, 11211.

OUR LADY OF MOUNT CARMEL
ROMAN CATHOLIC CHURCH

Reverend Peter Saponara was asked by Bishop John Loughlin to establish a neighborhood church for Italian immigrants to worship in their language. They gathered in Annunciation Church until they could dedicate their first building, Our Lady of Mount Carmel, in 1887.

The group began to celebrate the annual fiesta in July 1903, when the completion of the bridge brought legions of Lower East Side Italian immigrants to the area. Music, dance and food are reminders of the northern Italian village of Nola, where the feast of St. Paulinus was first celebrated in the sixteenth century. The giglio ("lily"), an eighty-five-foot-high painted spire holding the statue of Paulinus, is carried on the shoulders of more than two hundred participants. It is considered a rite of penance, an atonement that focuses on the physical stress of lifting the giglio, as well as a prayer of thanksgiving for faith and family.

Outgrowing its first church, the congregation planned another Italian Romanesque sanctuary during 1920 that would take ten years to complete, but it had the misfortune of being in the path of the Brooklyn-Queens Expressway and was demolished. The modern, golden-brick church erected in 1950 is a dramatic contrast to the neighborhood's older buildings and sits high on a plaza, with the BQE only a short distance away. Opaque-glass entrance doors hold colorful roundels of Christian symbols and lead into the serene wood-lined nave that seats more than six hundred. The baptismal font, with running water cascading into a marble pool, is placed at the entrance, signifying the rite of baptism as entry into Christian life. Be sure to visit the side chapel filled with polychrome statues of saints relevant to the Italian community and see the small plaque on the donor's board reminding visitors to "Do good and leave the rest to God."

275 North 8ᵗʰ Street (and Havemeyer Street), Brooklyn, NY 11211; 718-384-0223

RUSSIAN ORTHODOX CATHEDRAL OF THE TRANSFIGURATION OF OUR LORD

This Russian Byzantine church landmark, bordered by McCarren Park, was styled by Louis Allmendinger with five copper domes, octagonal belfries and twelve clerestory windows. The pale yellow brick façade features round exterior arches filled with stained glass, as well as the sculptured roundel of St. Vladimir that reads, "Equal to the Apostles Grand Prince of Kiev." Symbols of Eastern Orthodoxy, crosses with three horizontal bars, spring up from the domes like watchful guardians.

The congregation traces its roots to the area around the Carpathian Mountains in Russia and Poland. Services were first held in 1908 at the former Brooklyn Methodist Church on North 5ᵗʰ Street, which the group had dedicated to St. Vladimir, known as the enlightener of the Russian people. Outgrowing the space, the members acquired the present site bordering Greenpoint, with plans to replicate the Moscow Cathedral of the Assumption. Although started in 1916, construction was interrupted by World War I and was not completed until 1921.

The sanctuary is dedicated to the transfiguration on Mount Tabor, as told in the Bible. The sudden emanation of radiance from the body of Jesus, accompanied by Moses and Elijah, reassured his disciples that he was the Messiah. The gilded iconostatis, taken from the first church, was extended in

Russian Orthodox Cathedral of the Transfiguration of Our Lord.

1964 with images of Old Testament prophets to enhance the space. Look for a Russian icon from the first sanctuary, inscribed to the Russian Orthodox of Brooklyn and placed above the Royal Doors that lead into the main altar. See the painted images of archangels Michael and Gabriel and frescoes of Sts. Constantine and Helen, along with four other large murals: *The Nativity*, *The Protection of the Holy Virgin Mary*, *The Baptism of Jesus* and *The Resurrection*.

Many Orthodox groups stand for services, so you seldom find formal seating, but this congregation purchased secondhand pews in 1946 and can seat almost three hundred. English was introduced into the liturgy in about 1947, but with new Polish and Russian immigrants arriving, the language of the founding congregation continues to echo in the sanctuary.

228 North 12th Street (and Driggs Avenue), Brooklyn, NY 11211; 718-387-1064

Greenpoint

The Native American Leni-Lenape tribe once farmed, hunted and fished in this region, calling the area Green Hoek for its shoreline. By 1684, most of the land was controlled by Pieter Praa, a Dutch farmer whose descendants' names are on local street signs: Meserole, Calyer and Provost. Under British rule, the area would become known as Green Point.

As Brooklyn expanded, the Greenpoint-Williamsburg waterfront became a shipbuilding and manufacturing center. Corning Glass Works was started in 1823 as Brooklyn Flint Glass, while Charles Pratt (see Clinton Hill) established petroleum refineries in 1867. The local Continental Shipyard built the USS *Monitor*, the Union's first ironclad vessel launched for the Civil War in 1862.

In the 1880s, huge groups from Poland, Russia and Italy settled in the area, mixing with German, Irish and Scotch inhabitants. Today, it holds the largest concentration of Polish immigrants in New York, with local bridges honoring Polish patriots Tadeusz Kościuszko and Casimir Pulaski, both of whom joined with the colonists in 1776 during the Revolutionary War.

Overall, the neighborhood feels like a European village, with quiet blocks of private homes, access to the waterfront and ethnic shops alongside major brand stores lining Manhattan Avenue. Streets are named alphabetically from north to south, running from Ash to Quay Streets (Greenpoint Avenue replaces the letter "L" and Calyer Street the letter "P"). There are more than fourteen sacred havens, several parks and one surviving Jewish synagogue, a reminder of once thriving business owners who catered to waterfront industries.

In 1933, after one hundred years in operation, the last steamboat sailed from Greenpoint to Manhattan, signaling the end of its waterfront, but the area was slowly renewed by the influx of Polish immigrants and is now prime real estate.

McCARREN PARK

Straddling Greenpoint and Williamsburg, this thirty-six-acre park opened in 1936 and was named for local New York senator Patrick McCarren, who was the impetus behind the building of the Williamsburg Bridge. This landmark recreational space was always well utilized by the residents and includes a bathhouse with a pool that was damaged by fire in 1987 but is now restored. Sadly, the park lost its old trees to the Asian long-horned beetle in 1996, but replacements have begun to offer shady spots. With new housing springing up around its perimeter, McCarren Park continues to offer a peaceful place for neighborhood gatherings. It is located at Lorimer Street between Bayard Street and Driggs Avenue.

A smaller park nearby at Bedford and Nassau Avenues holds the Reverend Jerzy Popieluszko Memorial (1947–1984). He was a pro-democracy supporter murdered by Warsaw civil authorities during Poland's Solidarity movement. The textured stone monument in the shape of Poland is topped by a sculptured bust of the heroic young priest, whose sermons had been broadcasted by Radio Free Europe.

ST. STANISLAUS KOSTKA ROMAN CATHOLIC CHURCH

In 1875, St. Casimir's in Fort Greene was alone in offering Polish services, but as the immigrant community grew, so did its churches. In 1896, St. Casimir's pastor, Reverend Leon Wysiecki, founded two new parishes: Our Lady of Czenstochowa (see entry) and this national parish. During that time, the present site was in a German neighborhood. Following the church dedication in 1904, Germans left in large numbers as Polish immigrants arrived in even larger numbers. German members who remained in the parish donated a stained-glass window with the notation of "The German Catholics."

Today, the church is the largest Polish congregation in Brooklyn and continues the social and cultural traditions of Poland, celebrating *koleda*;

St. Stanislaus Kostka steeples.

the January Feast of the Three Kings; Pulaski Day; the signing of Poland's Constitution on May 3, 1791; and other national holidays. Church archives also recorded the congregation's support of those who struggled in Poland for survival during both world wars.

Two asymmetrical steeples dominate the skyline for miles, and when the Corrigan family of Russell Street wanted to know the time, they looked out their window to the steeple's clocks. Octagonal in shape and with ornamented spires, the tall towers crown an ornate Gothic sanctuary that seats more than 1,200 worshipers. Marble columns, gilded arches and stained-glass windows with images of saints relevant to the community enhance the nave, while a lavishly painted vaulted ceiling holds a choir of angels. Be sure to see an oil painting of the French Carmelite nun Theresa, who was canonized in 1926. The large canvas, created by Tadeusz Styka, visualizes the young saint's promise: "I will let fall from Heaven a shower of roses."

A revered portrait of the Black Madonna is prominently displayed on a side altar. Legend has it that the ancient icon of Mary, holding the young Jesus, is a source of miracles, a symbol of survival through Poland's dark days and a reminder of the indestructibility of the people's faith when fire destroyed their churches in World War II. Look for Patron Stanislaus (1550–1568) in two huge murals, one as a black-robed Jesuit tending to the poor and another as a young nobleman abandoning his affluent life to serve the people. Today, the church's street corners have been nicknamed "Lech Walesa Place," honoring the founder of the Solidarity movement and Poland's president in 1990, and "Pope John Paul II Plaza," commemorating the 1969 visit of Karol Cardinal Wojtyla of Krakow before his elevation as the first Polish pope. Both an interior portrait and an exterior bronze sculpture fondly recall the much-loved native son.

607 Humboldt Street (and Driggs Avenue), Brooklyn, NY 11222; 718-388-0170

JEHOVAH'S WITNESSES

This small modern chapel for the sect that preaches the Bible globally offers services in Polish, Spanish and English. The Brooklyn Heights worldwide headquarters (see entry) is in the process of relocating to upstate New York.

278 Driggs Avenue (and Leonard Street)

MONSIGNOR MCGOLDRICK PARK/WINTHROP PARK

Opened in the 1890s, this recreational space was named for local politician Winthrop Jones, who had secured financing for the almost ten-acre site. It was rededicated in 1941 to St. Cecilia's Roman Catholic Church's pastor, Edward J. McGoldrick (1857–1938), from County Donegal, Ireland, who had served the church and the community for fifty years. The well-utilized park holds several historical monuments: the landmark pavilion, with an elegant colonnade designed by Frank J. Helmle in 1910; the World War II *Winged Victory* bronze statue designed by Carl A. Heber in 1923, commemorating 150 local soldiers, as well as battle sites in France (Somme, Chateau Thierry and Argonne); and the 1939 *Monitor* monument by Antonio DeFillipo.

The ironclad *Monitor*, designed by John Ericsson for the Civil War, sailed from Greenpoint in January 1862 to battle the Southern vessel the *Merrimac*, a ship that was originally made in the North and known as the *Virginia*. The conflict took place off the shore of Hampton Roads in Virginia and ushered in the use of ironclad vessels over wooden ships. Neither side won,

The *Monitor* monument in McGoldrick Park.

and the *Monitor*, sinking in a storm off the coast of North Carolina, was recovered in 1973, with some artifacts eventually being displayed at the Brooklyn Historical Society. Look for a bronze tablet placed in the middle of a parking lot on West Street between Oak and Quay Streets marking the *Monitor* launch site. The Greenpoint *Monitor* Museum, founded in 1996 but without a permanent home, sponsors an annual parade and historical reenactment in period dress within the Church of the Ascension.

Driggs Avenue (and Russell Street)

St. Cecilia Roman Catholic Church

An Irish congregation, founded in 1871, built its first church on the site that would eventually become the school's gymnasium. During 1891, this massive Neo-Romanesque limestone church with corner bell tower and copper steeple was designed by Thomas H. Poole to seat eight hundred congregants. Having been restored in 1972, the interior glows with original wall colors, the Byzantine image of Christ in the apse and its marble reredos, filled with round arches and spires reflecting the exterior façade. See the stained-glass image of the piano-playing Cecilia, who was married against her wishes to Valerian, a non-Christian. Legend says that she took no part in her wedding festivities but instead sang to the Lord. On her wedding night, Cecilia told her husband that she had taken a vow of chastity, which he honored, and he, too, soon converted to Christianity. She was martyred upon her refusal to renounce her faith, and in many churches, you will find Cecilia's image placed in the choir loft. Once outside, walk up Russell Street to McGoldrick Park, named for the well-loved pastor who guided the flock for fifty years.

84 Herbert Street (and North Henry Street), Brooklyn, NY 11222; 718-389-0010

HOLY FAMILY ROMAN CATHOLIC SLOVAK CHURCH

This haven's cornerstone was dedicated in 1911 by Slovak immigrants from the Austro-Hungarian monarchy who founded their group in 1905. They had utilized St. Vincent de Paul Church (now demolished) and were committed to preserving their Slovak heritage and family culture. An appropriate mural of the Holy Family fills the interior apse. Sadly, the weathered red brick Romanesque building, whose corner tower is capped with a verdigris dome, sits alone in an area filled with vacant warehouses, and its former school is now a day-care center. The church has joined with the community in attempting to reclaim its shoreline, especially Newtown Creek, separating Brooklyn from Queens, whose waters have been destroyed by industrial pollution.

21 Nassau Avenue (and North 15th Street), Brooklyn, NY 11222; 718-388-5145

CHURCH OF THE ASCENSION

This Episcopal congregation, organized in 1846, built this English Gothic haven designed by Henry Dudley in 1865. Dudley was a favored architect of the Episcopal Diocese because of his ability to create serene sanctuaries recalling Anglican roots. A symmetrical façade of rock-faced granite has four lancet-shaped windows flanked by bright red doors that are topped with small oval windows. Enhanced by a garden and a black wrought-iron gate, the low-rise church adds a touch of country charm to its location amid vintage homes.

Thomas F. Rowland (1831–1907), the Continental Shipyard owner who engaged designer John Ericsson to build the ironclad *Monitor* for the Civil War, was a founding member and a major contributor to the church. An annual memorial service for Rowland, Ericsson and the crew of the *Monitor* is held in the intimate interior, which has an organ chamber adjoining the chancel. Participants re-create the time period in Civil War dress.

127 Kent Street (between Franklin and Manhattan Avenue), Brooklyn, NY 11222; 718-389-3831

CHURCH OF THE REDEEMER UNITED METHODIST (GREENPOINT POLISH AMERICAN UNITED METHODIST CHURCH)

In 1766, the first Methodist society was organized as a division of the Church of England in Lower Manhattan, but in keeping with the spirit of freedom that followed the American Revolution, the American Methodist Church was chartered in 1784. When the Greenpoint congregation opened this new haven in 1921 as the Corner Stone Temple Methodist Episcopal Church, its members also celebrated the seventy-fifth anniversary of Methodism in Brooklyn.

The congregation fell on hard times and shared the building with an English-language school. In 1993, the church was rescued by Reverend Richard Rutkowski, and its interior retains original stained glass, arch-styled pews and a wood-faced balcony. The pastor restored the apse with a white wooden podium that he handcrafted and placed a backlit cross within a shallow arch crowned with a triangular pediment. Polish immigrants who have helped in the restoration can hear the pastor's sermons in their native language.

112 Meserole Avenue (between Leonard and Manhattan), Brooklyn, NY 11222; 718-349-3628

ST. ANTHONY OF PADUA–ST. ALPHONSUS ROMAN CATHOLIC CHURCH

This German and Irish congregation was supported by Reverend Joseph Bronneman, who laid the foundation for this new parish in 1858 and named it for a fellow Franciscan. Members first held services in a small wooden church before they were able to finance this dramatic Gothic design, dedicated in 1874 and built by prolific Brooklyn architect Patrick C. Keely.

Gleaming white limestone highlights the red brick exterior, with its 240-foot gray shingled spire easily spotted in the community. Sculptured tympana, signed by the Sibbol Studio, include Jesus forgiving the prodigal son over one of three entrance doors. The interior sanctuary, 164 feet long and 72 feet wide, displays five murals that honor Patron Anthony (1195–1231), a nobleman born in Portugal who joined Francis of Assisi and became a brilliant preacher. He attacked the practice of usury and taught at universities in France and Padua, Italy, where he now perpetually rests.

An intimate tin ceiling chapel below the main sanctuary is open daily for a respite from noisy streets and has its own interesting artifacts and antique stained glass. The congregation of St. Alphonsus, founded in 1873 by German immigrants, merged with St. Anthony's in 1975. Its former brick church on Kent Street is now the Polish and Slavic Culture Center, which has preserved original stained-glass windows and its handsome steppe roof. Residential Milton Street bisects the commercial thoroughfare of Manhattan Avenue, giving residents on Milton Street a dramatic view of St. Anthony's well-preserved church.

862 Manhattan Avenue (and Milton Street), Brooklyn, NY 11222; 718-383-3339

BY THE WAY

St. John's Evangelical Lutheran Church, at 155 Milton Street (718-389-4012), has its German name, St. Johannes Kirche, etched over the entrance porch of the sanctuary, which was built in 1897. Surrounded by residential buildings, the red brick Gothic design by Theobald Engelhardt has a tall tower with copper steeple placed on the east side of the entrance, while a visible flying buttress reigns over the west.

Directly across the street at 136 Milton Street sits Greenpoint Reformed Church, which traces its roots to early Dutch settlers. It was built as a private home in 1866 for and by Thomas C. Smith. The red brick Italianate design has a simple white porch with pillars that are crowned by a triangular pediment. The two-storied bay-fronted building sits in a green garden enclosed by a high black wrought-iron fence. Interior woodwork, a tiled fireplace and plaster moldings remain from Smith, who owned the local Union Porcelain Works. The present congregation moved into the well-preserved space in 1944, adding stained-glass windows, one inscribed with "The Lord Is in His Holy Temple." The former church, St. Elias, is now closed and on the endangered list.

Sts. Cyril and Methodius Roman Catholic Church

Founded in 1917 as the Polish population continued to increase, this church was named for two sainted brothers from the ninth century. They were monks known as Apostles of the Slavs, patrons of the unity of the eastern and western church and creators of Cyrillic, the Russian alphabet. The modern, golden-brick Gothic church, which can seat six hundred, was built in 1951 and has small terra-cotta images of the patrons on either side of the entryway. The interior focuses on a white marble altar that glows with a mosaic of *The Last Supper* on its façade. Look in the balcony's stained-glass window to see the patrons preaching to the Slavic people.

150 Dupont Street (and Eagle Street), Brooklyn, NY 11222; 718-389-4424

Congregation Ahavas Israel

Congregation Ahavas Israel.

In 1893, Orthodox Ashkenazi founded this congregation and built this small Romanesque Revival synagogue in 1904, next door to the Reform temple of Congregation Beth El. While both remaining buildings share a common basement level, only Ahavas Israel (Love of Israel) holds services, and it is the last survivor of five synagogues that had resided in Greenpoint. As commercial industries left the area, so did families in the congregation. But their names would be permanently engraved on a white marble tablet in the narthex as a testament to their faith.

The narrow, cream-colored sanctuary, surrounded by a wood-faced balcony, holds two hundred worshipers. All eyes are drawn to the holy ark, guarded from above by golden Lions of Judah that flank gilded tablets of the Ten Commandments. A wheel window above the ark is filled with the stained-glass Shield of David outlined in red against a turquoise sky. Colorful stenciling surrounds the window and ceiling, while a dark wood bema, the reading table for the Torah scrolls, has brass menorahs on each corner. Look up to the barrel-shaped ceiling, pierced with three brightly colored oculi (skylights) and supporting an enormous Victorian chandelier with frosted-glass shades. Services are also conducted on the lower level under an original tin-paneled ceiling. When you leave, look for the Magen David (Shield of David) on the rooftop and see the icons repeated next door in the shuttered Beth El's stained-glass windows.

108 Noble Street (at Manhattan Avenue and Franklin Street), Brooklyn, NY 11222; 718-383-8475

Our tour is ended, but remember these havens continue to offer comfort and consolation in very tangible ways, and remain a source of hope amid the noise of this crowded city. They tell our stories, preserve our heritage and guide newcomers to prosperous and productive lives in America.

Metropolitan Transport Authority's New York City website: www.mta.info/nyct
Around-the-clock information: 718-330-1234
Non-English-speaking customers: 718-330-4847

Detailed neighborhood information available at www.mapquest.com

Appendix

Chronology

To understand why some havens are located in isolated or commercial areas, remember the major events that shaped Brooklyn's neighborhoods.

1638   Native Americans surrender lands (Greenpoint, Williamsburg and Bushwick) to Dutch West India Company.

1646   Town of Breuckelen charter set up for Dutch West India Company.

1654   Flatbush Dutch Reformed Church is founded as the first church in Brooklyn.

1664   New Amsterdam is renamed New York after British conquest.

1776   The Battle of Brooklyn is fought along the coastline. General George Washington retreats with the colonial army. British troops remain until 1783.

1801   The Navy Yard opens on Wallabout Bay, starting an economic boom.

1814   The steamboat *Nassau*, Robert Fulton's invention, is a faster link between Manhattan and Brooklyn. Both cities have Fulton Street Terminals. Fulton dies in 1815 and today rests at Trinity Church in Manhattan.

1825   The Erie Canal links New York Harbor to the Great Lakes. Brooklyn ports expand.

1834   The towns of New Amersfoort (Flatlands), Midwout (Flatbush), Boswick (Bushwick), Gravesend and New Utrecht merge with the town of Brooklyn, which will grow to the third-largest city in America.

1841   First publication of daily newspaper, the *Brooklyn Eagle*, lasting until 1955. The American poet of Democracy, Walt Whitman, will serve as editor (1846–48).

Appendix

1848   Brooklyn City Hall (Borough Hall) is inaugurated as government center.

1850   The Great Atlantic Docks, with room for 150 ships, open in Red Hook.

1862   The ironclad *Monitor*, built and launched in Greenpoint, departs for the Civil War.

1867   Prospect Park provides a huge recreational space.

1868   Eastern Parkway becomes the world's first six-lane thoroughfare.

1880   Thomas Edison introduces the electric light.

1883   The Brooklyn Bridge links with New York City, the country's largest city.

1897   Brooklyn Public Library and Brooklyn Museum of Art in Prospect Heights are constructed.

1898   The "Twin Cities," Brooklyn and New York, merge on January 1.

1903   Williamsburg Bridge's completion attracts settlers from Lower East Side.

1908   IRT (New York's first subway) connects corridor to Brooklyn. Brooklyn Academy of Music from 1859 relocates to Fort Greene.

1909   Manhattan Bridge links busy Canal Street and Flatbush Avenue.

1911   Brooklyn Botanic Garden makes debut in Prospect Heights.

1924   Ferry terminals become obsolete due to automobile, introduced in 1908.

1929   Williamsburgh Bank Tower becomes Brooklyn's first skyscraper at 512 feet.

1931   Floyd Bennett Field, built on landfill, is dedicated as New York City's first airport.

1936   IND Subway opens to Brooklyn.

1950   Brooklyn Battery Tunnel and Brooklyn-Queens Expressway destroy neighborhood streets, sacred havens and private homes during construction.

1964   Verrazano-Narrows Bridge connects Brooklyn to Staten Island.

1965   New York City Landmarks Preservation Commission is established. Brooklyn Heights is designated as the first historic district due to community activism.

1972   Gateway Recreation Area, created by the National Park Service, is established, including southeastern Floyd Bennett Field.

1998   MetroTech/Renaissance Plaza, with Marriott Hotel, renews downtown.

2001   Brooklyn Bridge is used as an escape route when the World Trade Center, which opened in 1973, is destroyed by a terrorist attack on 9/11.

2012   Brooklyn continues to gentrify: Barclays Center sports arena transforms Atlantic Avenue.

Index

INDEX

INDEX

INDEX

About the Author

Terri Cook is a native New Yorker and New York University graduate. She currently works as a marketing consultant and tour guide, shining a spotlight on New York's cultural heritage. She is the author of *Sacred Havens: A Guide to Manhattan's Spiritual Places*.